OPEN-PLAN OFFICES

OPEN-PLAN OFFICES

by Axel Boje Dipl.Kfm.

Edited by B. H. Walley

Business Books Limited · London

First published 1968 by Verlag Moderne Industrie
Wolfgang Dummer & Co., München 23, under the title
Das Grossraum Büro
English edition first published 1971

ISBN 0 220 66768 3

This book has been set in 11 on 13 pt Baskerville 169 and
printed in England by The Camelot Press Ltd., London and Southampton,
for the publishers, Business Books Limited
(Registered office: 180 Fleet Street, London EC4)
Publishing offices: Mercury House, Waterloo Road, London SE1

MADE AND PRINTED IN GREAT BRITAIN

Contents

Part B Contributions from firms with open-plan offices
Edited by Axel Boje

Part C Symposium
Edited by Axel Boje

List of plates

Preface to the English edition

The term *Bürolandschaft* must be one of the few German words which
has become established in the British lexicon of management terms
during the last few years. This surely must denote a keen interest in
office landscaping and its association with the open-plan office. Regret-
fully it also rightly suggests that Germany has been ahead of UK
practice in this field.

In Western Germany Axel Boje is the foremost consultant concerned
with the open-plan office technique and as this edited translation shows
his conclusions have been drawn from experience in over a thousand
concerns.

Both the application and results of introducing open-plan offices in
Germany may have a greater relevance to the UK than have similar
experiences in the USA. The two European countries are comparative
late-comers to the use of open-plan offices; both are tending to apply
office landscaping to the technique, and of course each country has an
innate conservatism, especially among clerical workers, which is perhaps
not so prevalent in the USA.

Axel Boje has made an excellent case for the consideration and the
eventual introduction of open-plan offices. The factors in their favour
seem overwhelming. Yet there are several additional facets which
should be considered.

Despite the Offices Act and the tremendous amount of office building
which has taken place in central London, the over-all standard of office
accommodation in the UK is still not high. A new open-plan office will
obviously be attractive if the previous office accommodation was
dingy, full of antiquated furniture or badly planned.

The subsequent increase in office productivity which Axel Boje
suggests is an important factor in deciding upon the adoption of the
open-plan office, can only be proved if clerical work measurement has
been undertaken both before and after the change in office layout. Few
companies in the UK would even now have the requisite work measurement data to support claims for increased productivity in the office.

Morale is an important element in assessing the desirability of introducing open-plan offices and the answers to questionnaires given in the book try to show this. Morale is a difficult thing to measure and though it certainly can be affected by general office conditions, the major influences on morale may be inherent in the company itself—in the way it is managed, in pay rates, in company discipline and work schedules. Office conditions may only be a minor factor in influencing the morale of the clerical work force. Attitudes about the open-plan office may be influenced accordingly.

This point will also have a direct bearing on the effect of psychological conditioning given prior to the introduction of an open-plan office.

These comments do not greatly detract from the case for the open-plan office. Obviously, company tradition and general managerial conservatism will prevent the rapid adoption of such an environment, but many of the largest companies in the UK are now considering its practicability. Some—BP, Unilever, Boots—have excellent examples of this genre. This trend can only continue.

Prefix to the English edition

Some of the terms used in this book, particularly measurement terminology, may be unfamiliar to British readers. The most important terms are explained below.

Phons and bels

Throughout the book the acoustic measurement used is phons, where normally decibels (dB) or bels, i.e. 10 dB, are used in this country. The two are not really comparable.

Phons are units of loudness of sound output as it affects the human ear, and in order to provide a measurement for comparison purposes when using such a dimensionless unit a Sone Scale was devised to give numbers proportional to loudness level, viz:

$$S = 2^{(P-40)/10}$$

Using logarithms to the base 2 this formula is more easily handled in the form

$$P = 40 + 10 \log_2 S$$

Bels, or decibels, are used when referring to sound rating or as a reduction coefficient of sound. An inside level of Noise (N_i) is said to be separated by B bel from an outside noise level (N_o) providing

$$B = \log_{10}\left(\frac{N_i}{N_o}\right)$$

So to reduce an outside noise level of N_o to an acceptable level of N_i inside a building, the formula quoted will give the sound rating in bels (or 10 dB)*.

Lux and lumen

Metrication is impinging further and further on the measurement of illumination levels. Recently the Illuminating Engineering Society

* Confirmed with the Manchester Building Design Centre.

(York House, Westminster Bridge Road, London SE1) published a new edition of the IES Code. The new code is a metric publication and recommends various changes in the measurement of lighting quality.

The publication uses the Systeme International d'Unites (SI). All measurements are derived from the six basic units—metres (length and width), kilogramme (mass), second (time), ampere (current), degree Kelvin (absolute temperature) and candela (luminous intensity).

The Systeme International's unit of luminous flux remains the lumen (lm), but the unit of illumination is the lux (lx) which is 1 lm/m²; 10·76 lx equals 1 lm/ft².

Evaporated gold film

The German term, *Goldbedampfung*, evaporated gold film, refers to a fairly standard technique in which thin evaporated metal films on glass are used to reduce heat loss or gain through radiation. Cost and stability are the main factors inhibiting its widespread use.*

Metric conversions

$$1 \text{ m} = 3 \cdot 281 \text{ ft}$$
$$1 \text{ m}^2 = 10 \cdot 765 \text{ ft}^2$$
$$10 \text{ m}^2 = 107 \cdot 65 \text{ ft}^2$$
$$100 \text{ m}^2 = 1{,}076 \cdot 496 \text{ ft}^2$$
$$1{,}000 \text{ m}^2 = 10{,}765 \text{ ft}^2$$
$$1{,}500 \text{ m}^2 = 16{,}147 \text{ ft}^2$$
$$2{,}000 \text{ m}^2 = 21{,}530 \text{ ft}^2$$
$$2{,}500 \text{ m}^2 = 26{,}912 \text{ ft}^2$$
$$3{,}000 \text{ m}^2 = 32{,}295 \text{ ft}^2$$
$$3{,}500 \text{ m}^2 = 37{,}677 \text{ ft}^2$$
$$4{,}000 \text{ m}^2 = 43{,}060 \text{ ft}^2$$
$$4{,}500 \text{ m}^2 = 48{,}442 \text{ ft}^2$$
$$5{,}000 \text{ m}^2 = 53{,}825 \text{ ft}^2$$
$$6{,}000 \text{ m}^2 = 64{,}590 \text{ ft}^2$$
$$7{,}000 \text{ m}^2 = 75{,}355 \text{ ft}^2$$
$$8{,}000 \text{ m}^2 = 86{,}120 \text{ ft}^2$$
$$9{,}000 \text{ m}^2 = 96{,}885 \text{ ft}^2$$

* Confirmed with the Professor of Building Science, University of Liverpool.

Part A

FEATURES, ORGANIZATION AND PROFITABILITY

by Axel Boje

Chapter 1

What is an open-plan office?

An open-plan office is a place in which office work is performed, its size being a multiple of the smallest possible unit of floor space.

The synonym 'open-office area' [1, p 18] emphasizes the spatial conception and configuration of the open area as an architectural planning exercise in ground plan, outer fabric, inside fittings and technical maintenance. (In the industrial field there are also in addition to open-office areas, open storage, conference, selling, counter, filing and other areas.) The choice of the term 'open-office area' stresses the idea of the technical form and layout of such an area*.

The term 'open-plan office', which is just as widely used in literature (see [1] and the works of Alsleben, Gottschalk, Hess, Schnelle, Weltz and others listed in the Bibliography) and speech, shifts the emphasis to office work and to the functions to be performed in the open area. Moreover, the origin of the German word for 'office' (*Büro*†) indicates a fundamental connection between function and room. The room is a means of optimizing office work. Since the open-plan office exists side by side with the closed-plan office, and the multi- with the single-person office, the questions must be asked: 'Which type of room provides the optimum geographical, technical, organizational and economic conditions for the performance of office work? Does the open-plan office offer the most economical use of space for office work? (This term relates the service and working areas to the office function. In this sense, therefore, the term open-plan office is preferred to open-office area in the following pages.)

The German term *Funktionsbüro*‡ likewise means the spatial

---

* The publications largely relating to technical aspects and sometimes extended to include physiological effects, e.g. [2].

† From Latin *burrus* (dark and dismal colour) from which the old French *la bure* (table-covering for official public proceedings), then extended to mean the whole, *le bureau* (desk, bureau). Thus the modern German word *Büro* is a comprehensive term covering all work of an office nature carried out at a desk.

‡ On the one hand the German word *Büro* already includes the concept of a work function, and the term *Funktionsbüro* is therefore a tautological expression, and on the other the intended open-area content is not expressed in the word *Funktionsbüro*. A

configuration related to the work to be performed, without making this concept adequately clear. 'Landscaped office' [3], whilst indicating the extended area, also conjures up the landscaped idea of an office space with plants, room-dividing elements, freely distributed areas for workplaces, furniture and traffic aisles. There is some justification for promoting the landscaped office as an indispensable attribute [3] of an optimum open-office area, but not for confusing landscaped offices and open-plan offices or open-office areas [4]. Even an open-office area which is not designed as a landscape must unquestionably be recognized as an open-plan office. There is no doubt that productive work has been and is being carried out [5] in open-office areas parsimoniously designed, in landscaped-office terms, in the USA at present, in France, Italy, the Iron-curtain countries, Japan and South Africa, in West Germany and in Germany before 1918. Even poorly endowed openoffice areas deserve to be called open-plan offices and share many of the advantages of modern open-plan offices of 'landscaped' conception. The landscaped office is a particular form of open-office area, which has long been, under central European conditions, the optimum solution from the technical, aesthetic, organizational and economic point of view. Nevertheless it is not correct to include this or any other specific form of internal design as an indispensable feature of the term 'open-plan office'.

1.1 Size

There are various opinions as to the lower and upper size limits for the open-plan office. The following suggestions for the minimum size of an open-plan office are based on personal practical experience:

Tiedemann	from 160 m² (16 workplaces)
Henn	from 200 m² (1955)
	from 600 m² (1964)
Boje	from 200 m²
Fischer, M.	from 250–3,000 m²
Reznik	from 324 m² (18 × 18 m)
DAG (Deutsche Angestellten-Gewerkschaft)	from 400 m² (20 × 20 m)
Schmallenbach-Gesellschaft	from 400–1,300 m²
Gottschalk	from 600–1,000 m²

closed-plan office may be covered by the term *Funktionsbüro* because functions are performed or work can be carried out functionally therein.

4

Dr Schmidt [6], organization director of Bertelsmann Verlag (Gütersloh), who has experience of various open-plan systems up to a maximum size of 2,500 m², specifies 3,000 m² as a minimum area for an open-plan office.

Funke [7, p 12] takes the size of the area into account in his definition of open plan, and requires a minimum size of 600 m² and a minimum width of 20 m at any given point (although the open-plan areas of Fried. Krupp (Rheinhausen) and Helmut Horten GmbH (Düsseldorf) are only 15 m wide and are accepted by Funke as open-plan areas) and a minimum capacity of 80 persons (7·6 m² per person).

All the minimum-size theories suggested previously have remained unproven. The same applies to the 200 m² minimum proposed by the author. The economic costs and output factors presented by the author in this work are valid for open-office areas of at least 200 m²; in smaller areas the costs are higher and the output is lower. In open-office areas of 400, 600 and 800 m² and over, the output figures are only slightly higher and the costs only slightly lower than with floor areas of 200 m² so there is no point in ascertaining individual profitability figures for the larger areas. The sharp drop in output and rise in costs in the case of an office area of less than 200 m² confirms the author's opinion, expressed as long ago as 1956, that an open-office area offers economic advantages over the closed-plan office only starting from a size of approximately 200 m². Nevertheless, the 'small open-office area' requires a slightly higher relative expenditure for sound-proofing measures than the medium or large office area in order to obtain equal or at least similar output results.

As these figures show, there are also differences of opinion as to the economically sound upper limit for the open-plan office with variations of 1,000–3,000 m². There have been plans for areas of up to 9,000 m², but they have not materialized as yet. Hermkes [8] is of the opinion that the open-office area should not be larger than 2,000 m², but does not give reasons for this figure.

The optimum floor area depends, of course, on whether the office premises are to be built in a single plane, as several vertical open areas or as a high block with correspondingly smaller open areas. Several factors influence the optimum floor area and hence ground plan and type of building.

The first consideration is the total area required. The following factors should be determined in each case to act as mathematical parameters: distance between floors (3·40–4·80 m over-all dimension), number of lifts, speed of lifts (including braking and accelerating time), frequency of lift stops (frequency of lift usage), average duration of lift stops (number of persons entering and leaving) and walking speed in the horizontal plane. On the basis of these technical and therefore generally applicable criteria, the optimum floor area has been ascertained for the first time (by the staff of Axel Boje Unternehmungsberatung, Düsseldorf) by means of a mathematical model (see Appendix 1). Starting with the conditions of a practical example having a total area of 50,000 m² the optimum floor area of one storey proved to be 1,176 m². Meanwhile other calculations made by this method for different total areas and similar technical conditions have given optimum storey floor areas of approximately the same order. The following assumption can be made from these experiments: solely on the basis of present-day technical performance data for overcoming horizontal and vertical distances, the figures for an optimum storey floor area in an open-plan office is 1,000–1,300 m². This area is related to one central set of services, i.e. to one technical core. If there are two technical cores, the optimum storey floor area is doubled, i.e. 2,000–2,600 m². The above-mentioned optimum floor area of one storey is thus always to be understood as an office area designed centripetally around a single technical core. (A technical core consists of services such as lifts, stairways, rest rooms, toilet facilities, etc.—*Tech. Ed.*)

In these calculations, economic factors such as property prices, building costs for low and high buildings, costs for lifts, stairs and conveyors, and salary costs for office staff, have been disregarded. When property prices are very high, the optimum floor area figure drops; when they are low (for example on the outskirts of towns or in the provinces), it rises. With high salary costs and low density of internal traffic, the optimum floor area tends towards the lower limit, and with high density of traffic is somewhat higher. With low salary costs and low density of traffic, the optimum figure lies in the middle, at about 1,200 m², and under the same conditions with high density of traffic is in the region of the upper limit (1,300 m² and over). These economic data can be less easily generalized as regards geographical location or prevailing conditions. The following rule of thumb has evolved from existing plans and building constructions: in the centre of large towns the technical and economic optimum storey floor area is of the order of 300–800 m²; in peripheral zones and the provinces it stands at about 800–1,400 m.²

1.2 Optimum features of the open-plan office

Although even the poorly equipped area merits the term open plan by virtue of its size and function, only those having optimum technical, functional and economic features are worthy of interest. The features of such an optimum open-plan office are summarized in the following pages and must be considered as indispensable conditions if one is to justify the economic superiority of the open-plan office over its closed-plan equivalent.

The area comprising the open-plan office should not be absolutely open and fully visible; it must be sub-divided by screens, partitions, furniture, cloakrooms, counters and other fittings. The screens and partitions should be interchangeable and not reach to the ceiling; a height of up to 1·60 m is sufficient. Without an air-conditioning plant the open-plan office is not at its best. Natural ventilation via windows causes draughts, frequent changes in temperature, and introduces dust and external noise. These disadvantages are obviated by air-conditioning, although, according to present experiences, air-conditioning plants need a year's running-in before becoming fully operationally efficient. Moreover, too intensive a circulation of air should be avoided because of the creation of draughts.

Optimum sound-absorbing measures are an indispensable condition of open-plan offices. These include fitted carpets, acoustic ceilings (possibly with sound-absorbing panels) and sound-absorbing wall linings. Even the partitions should, if possible, be covered with sound-deadening material. The glass content of the area should be kept as low as possible. Curtains may assist the sound-absorbing effect.

Lighting must give conditions at least equivalent to natural light and, if possible, better. It should be uniform and non-glare, functional, output-promoting and non-injurious to health. It can be predominantly artificial.

As free a distribution of work positions and fittings as possible will avoid the character of a mass workroom, which is not popular in central Europe. A free, asymmetrical arrangement of work positions serves this purpose. Plant tubs, plant racks, aquaria [9] and other pleasing spatial elements soften the working atmosphere and create the character of an office landscape.

The open-plan area must be provided with equipment that can fulfil the requirements of working and living. This means a compact array of electrical connections in the floor or ceiling (2–3 m intervals), toilets and washrooms, cloakrooms, storage places for cleaning materials, and above all a rest room, in which employees can relax and refresh themselves during freely organized break periods. Comfortable seats, pleasant furnishings, kitchen facilities for the preparation of hot and cold drinks, the installation of beverage vending machines and the like, all have a place. Recently these facilities are being extended to include separate 'siesta' rooms where employees can lie down, and also powder rooms. The 'siesta' room not only enables the tired worker to have a refreshing nap, but may also provide the expectant mother with a much-needed rest on a couch. Another output-related feature is a keep-fit room, where a tape-recorder playing music and exercising instructions can be switched on to provide five minutes of programmed exercises, which are very relaxing and produce a feeling of well-being. This can be of immediate value in increasing output, particularly in the case of clerical staff, punched card operators, sedentary women workers, expectant mothers and those with back-ache or other sedentary complaints.

Equipped with such features the open-office area provides the most favourable conditions for optimum work performance. An area designed in this way offers all the advantages of a modern open-plan office.

The most important functional feature of the open-plan office is flexibility. Internal flexibility over the largest possible floor area permits any desired arrangement of work positions and sub-divisions with as frequent changes as required. When it is merely necessary to shift movable screens, storage units and the like, heavy conversion costs are avoided. There should, if possible, be a corresponding external flexibility, i.e. the possibility of extending the existing ground plan outwards, which is more readibly feasible in low buildings than in high ones. It is then possible to arrange work areas from a functional aspect, i.e. according to the type and extent of the work involved. The conventional school-room arrangement gives way to continuous production lines, centrally related circular arrangements, groupings of two or more persons, and other forms.

Sound-absorbing room fittings, full air-conditioning and daylight-independent lighting ensure undisturbed work. At the same time there is optimum information flow unhindered by doors and unnecessarily long distances. The advantages of a close communication network are thus combined with conditions necessary for undisturbed, concentrated work. The numerous fittings satisfy physiological and psychological human requirements.

Even the Deutsche Angestellten-Gewerkschaft (German Employees Union), which was initially sceptical about the open-plan development, has since given frequent recognition to the open-plan office and has drawn up nine requirements for its design [10]:

1 Area size at least 20 × 20 m (400 m²).
2 Each work position 8 m², plus reserve.
3 Full air-conditioning with protection against heat radiation.
4 Non-glare and shadow-free lighting, colour of light adapted to daylight.
5 Depth of noise up to 50 phon; range of understanding of conversations up to 5 m; noise-generating machines to be installed so that, as far as possible, sound is absorbed.
6 Colour-muted and sound-proofed furniture; demarcation of aisles and work positions.
7 Open, asymmetrical, movable furnishings and fittings.
8 Rest rooms, if possible with access to outside.
9 Employees' representatives to be positively consulted before and during the planning stage (in accordance with S 66, 1b, S 73 Pers VG, S 72 Betr VG).

1.3 For whom is the open-plan office suitable?

There is no activity concerned with the administration of an undertaking that could not be carried out in an open-plan office. Nevertheless not every administrative function can be performed with optimum results in an open-plan office, and not every person produces his best output in such an office.

The open-plan office is suitable for commercial, industrial, administrative and scientific concerns, but with exceptions. Such exceptions, for example, are certain ministries and government offices in which employees carry out confidential tasks and where not only the desk but the whole room must be lockable to prevent unauthorized access to exposed documents and files. Otherwise, open-plan offices can be set up with economic effect in central and local government departments, professional organizations and centralized head offices, all industrial and commercial concerns, banks, insurance companies, publishing firms, service departments and all other administrative concerns.

The open-plan office can be used with full economic effect for creative and repetitive work, for directive and executive functions, for management and general duties, for both sexes, for any age group, for any nationality or for any other human group. There are a few exceptions to the functions to which it is applicable, and for which the open-plan office is not recommended, namely:

1 The performance of confidential work.
2 The fulfilment of prestige obligations.
3 Where there are a large number of visitors to part of the open-office area or particularly conspicuous visitors.
4 Where the users of the office have to speak very loudly.
5 Jobs requiring extreme and undisturbed concentration.

In such exceptional cases the closed plan, i.e. the single room, is to be preferred.

The single room ensures that conversations are absolutely confidential and it prevents access to documents and files, which can be had very easily in an open-plan office. This does not mean that confidential work could not, in many cases, be performed in open-plan offices—for instance the personnel division is sometimes incorporated within the open-plan office, e.g. Schmalbach (Brunswick) and Horten (Düsseldorf).

Prestige requirements can be fulfilled on a larger scale in the closed-plan office than in an open-plan office. The closed office provides walls for wood panelling, inlays and paintings and allows individual decoration with expensive vases and porcelain. In addition, the exclusive character is enhanced by the seclusion. Nevertheless, the open-plan office also allows the hanging of paintings at certain places, e.g. Nino (Nordhorn), and the laying of oriental carpets to add prestige. A large number of visitors is not disturbing in an open-plan office if it affects all departments equally. If visitor traffic is directed only to certain sectors, it is very disturbing to the adjacent working sections. Visitors who are conspicuous by their personal identity, colour, clothes or behaviour, create a considerable disturbance for all persons working within visible range. Such streams of visitors should be kept out of open-plan offices, screened off by solid-walled corridors and received in isolated rooms.

As yet telephonic communications are not free of disturbance and lack the desirable technical precision which would allow quiet telephone conversation in all cases. Perpetual loud speaking on the telephone is unavoidable for many desk users. Such employees must be prevented from disturbing their neighbours by enclosure within sound-absorbing walls. They must have single rooms.

Creative work at the highest stage of concentration is only possible in the complete absence of outside stimuli and interference. Here again, a single room can be conceded. This exception, however, must be adapted to the personality of the user. Many creative minds need a certain minimum of acoustic and visual disturbance to be able to work concentratedly*. This is proved, for example, by the libraries and study rooms of universities, where academic work is carried out although a certain low noise level (of up to 10 phon) and occasional non-stimulating movements exert a slightly disturbing influence. The single room with absolute freedom from disturbance may, because of its complete lack of stimuli, detract from the mentally creative worker's alertness and his ability to concentrate on the task in hand. Tests have proved, e.g. BH (Hamburg), that highly expert and mentally creative work in management departments, for example, can be carried out in open-plan offices with an output at least equivalent to that of the enclosed office.

It has been proved that up to 80 highly qualified staff in a legal department dealing with accountancy, inland revenue and organization have carried out their work with at least average efficiency in an open-plan office. On the other hand there are concerns that have erected administrative blocks of closed-plan offices for their chief administrative division. This consisted almost exclusively of management departments, which preferred single rooms in most cases, e.g. Rheinstahl (Essen).

There still remains within the open-plan office one possibility of improving on the general spatial conditions for individual concentrated work: the concentrated work point. This consists of a single table-type desk and chair and is placed at any desired point in the open-office area for free use by anyone. There is no telephone on the desk, so that the user is not available for communication purposes, but neither can he be disturbed.

The machine room of an EDP (Electronic Data Processing) unit requires a special floor construction because of the cabling, separate air-conditioning and fire precautions, differing from the normal office type. For these reasons an EDP machine room, although, of course, it may be designed as an open-plan office in itself, must be clearly separated from the open area of all other office departments. Walls should reach to the ceiling although these should still be sectional. A separate records room is also advisable for the storage of tapes and discs

* Manfred Fischer recommends for management, research and development work, single rooms which are free of any optical or acoustic disturbance [11].

11

and possibly also for punched cards. Office areas for punched card operators, data preparation, systems analysts and planners, programmers and other EDP personnel (apart from the machine operators) can be incorporated without any particular difficulty in the normal open-plan office.

1.4 Where are there open-plan offices?

Open-plan offices falling within the definition on which this work is based are more widely distributed than is generally supposed. In other countries, moreover, the erection of open-plan offices does not meet with the same antagonism as in Germany. In the USA the majority of all large commercial and administrative concerns are equipped with open-plan offices, and up to the present there has been no indication of a general reversal of this trend. In Japan open-plan offices are very common for administrative concerns. In South Africa open-plan offices are the rule in banks and insurance companies, and exist in small numbers in industry. In England they are rare, in France and Switzerland they are to be found occasionally, and in Italy they are widespread.

In West Germany an investigation by Schmalenbach-Gesellschaft [12, p 12] in 1960 into 19 office buildings [1, pp 22 and 30]* (doubtless so small a number cannot claim to be representative) defined by this company as having 'modern organization', showed the percentage distributions in Table 1.1. The researchers deduced from this

Table 1.1

Number of occupants	Offices, %	Employees, %
1 or 2	64	43
3 or 4	24	29
5 to 9	10	22
10 and over	2	6
Total	100	100

study that large offices occupied by 10 or more persons have no role in Germany.

The author considers it questionable whether one can draw from investigations into 19 office buildings such a generalized conclusion for

* As late as 1965 the authors generalize the results of this very small cross-sectional study and identify the 1960 results with conditions in 1965 [1, p 30].

the total of approximately 200,000 large and small concerns in West Germany. From the author's personal experience and observations in more than 1,000 concerns, the distribution of open-plan offices in the Federal Republic of Germany can be calculated as shown in Table 1.2.

Table 1.2

Type of concern	Number of concerns		Open-plan offices		Persons in open-plan offices	
	Approximate total	Approximate number with open plan	Per concern	Total	Per open-plan office	Total
Insurance companies	300	80	5	400	60	24,000
Banks and savings banks*	17,000	250	2	500	40	20,000
Warehousing and distribution companies	5,000	20	5	100	40	4,000
Wholesalers	10,000	10	1	10	30	300
Industry:						
Large concerns†	1,000	80	4	320	60	19,000
Medium concerns†	9,000	20	1	20	50	1,000
Small concerns†	92,000	200	1	200	20	4,000
Authorities:						
Federal and State	5,000	40	2	80	20	1,600
Municipal	42,000	300	1	300	20	6,000
Other	20,000	200	1	200	20	4,000
Totals	201,300	1,200		2,130		83,900

* Including branches.

† Large concerns—over 2,000 employees; medium concerns—250–2,000 employees; small concerns—up to 250 employees.

With approximately 84,000 office employees in West Germany working in more than 2,000 open-plan offices, the type of office layout can scarcely be considered an insignificant contemporary phenomenon or a disturbing element. In banks and insurance companies in particular it has long been the accepted thing for office work to be performed in open-plan offices. The open-plan office existed even at the turn of the century, e.g. Siemens (Berlin) and Borsig, and can be traced back as far as the Middle Ages, to the counting houses of merchants [13].

Open-plan offices of modern conception with the features mentioned in Section 1.2 have evolved only in the last ten years and for the time being constitute less than 5 per cent of all existing open-plan offices in the Federal Republic of Germany. There is therefore no justification for anxiety in the face of an unknown phenomenon—either as regards the old-fashioned or the modern, ideally designed, open-plan office. The position is also affected by a mental predisposition towards the conventional closed office (by no means an exclusively German phenomenon). Human beings do not yield naturally to reason and expediency or to economic considerations. A typical example of this mentality is to be found in the results of an inquiry set up at Helmut Horten GmbH, (Düsseldorf) before the construction of an open-plan office. According to the wishes of the staff, rooms should be occupied as follows:

69 per cent by 1 person.
10 per cent by 2 persons.
6·5 per cent by 3 persons.
5 per cent by 4 persons.
9·5 per cent by 5 or more persons.

Helmut Horten did not follow the majority wishes of the 800 office workers who were swayed by their emotions; they acted rationally for economic reasons. There seems little point in asking people for their opinions about a state of affairs of which they have no first-hand knowledge. Inquiries directed at users of open-plan offices with adequate personal experience yield a quite different picture, as proved for example by a questionnaire issued by the DIB—Deutsche Institut für Betriebswirtschaft (German Institute of Management)—Frankfurt am Main, on the occasion of a Conference of Organizers in 1966:

Good experience of an open-plan office: 89 per cent of users of open-plan offices.

Good impression of open-plan offices inspected: 75 per cent of those inspecting them.

Own work position in an open-plan office: 60 per cent of the participants (120 organizers).

Permanently in favour of open-plan offices: 68 per cent of the participants.

Even employees who, prior to their own experience of open-plan offices, are against them, come to accept them after a period of six to eight months of getting used to them, and recognize their numerous advantages*. This does not mean unreserved enthusiasm for the open-plan office in every case. It is still hard to dispel a latent wish for the closed office or single room amongst office workers of West and Central Germany, even though experience and inspection have at least overcome a declared antagonism to the open-plan office, in users of well-designed open-plan areas.

One cannot conceal the fact that many concerns have had negative experiences with open-plan offices. For example, four well-known large concerns in Hanover, Ingelheim, Mainz and Ludwigshafen originally set up open-plan offices, only to reconvert them into closed offices six months to eleven years later, as a result partly of massive opposition by their staff and partly of objective functional disadvantages. How decisive individual sociological claims are in the choice of the closed type of office is proved by the case of a large pharmaceutical concern in South Baden, where the higher ranking doctors and chemists were allocated closed offices as status symbols, whilst the lower ranking commercial staff (accounts, buying, sales and other departments) were accommodated in open-plan offices. One large concern in Cologne suffered a general skin-rash outbreak on fitting out an air-conditioned high building with open-plan offices. Most of the office employees developed the complaint, the reason for which was sought in vain in the air-conditioning plant, the desk tops, electrostatic voltage fields, and in biological and psychological circumstances. It disappeared three months later as mysteriously as it had come.

Such negative experiences should not be used as a general argument against the open-plan office. Poor experience with open-plan offices—with constant conditions during the period of use—can nearly always be traced to faulty planning and direction. In such cases those responsible have not observed the following rules:

1 An open-plan office should be used only where a definite purpose is served. Careful organizational and architectural planning should supply the basis for an objective decision on open versus closed plan. The open-plan office should not be dogmatically and universally enforced without taking all factors into consideration.

2 An objectively reached decision to have open-plan offices must be carried into effect consistently without signs of self-doubt. Lack of self-confidence or disagreement at the decision stage promotes and nourishes opposition.

* See open-plan office test in this book.

3 The office area must be ideally designed as regards size and fittings. False economy leads to considerable output losses and often to a failure of the open-plan office.

4 The staff should be promptly and fully informed of the decision to have an open-plan office and psychologically prepared for the new spatial and working conditions. Limited collaboration of the staff in the detailed planning (arrangement of workplaces, design of workplaces, decoration) may be useful.

5 Patience and firmness during the initial difficulties. Any objectively recognizable faults should be remedied quickly and effectively.

Without appraisal we list the following West German concerns which have set up open-plan offices in the last ten years and had predominantly good experiences:

    1 Allianz-Versicherungs-AG, München

    2 Anker-Werke AG, Bielefeld (Abt. Kundendienst)

    3 Bertelsmann Verlagsgemeinschaft GmbH, Rheda

    4 Bochumer Verein AG, Bochum

    5 C. F. Boehringer & Söhne, Mannheim

    6 Böllhof, Brackwede

    7 BP Benzin und Petroleum AG, Hamburg

    8 BV-Aral, Bochum

    9 Friedrich Deckel, Maschinenbau, München

  10 Deutscher Adressbuch-Verlag, Darmstadt

  11 Deutscher Ring, Versicherungs-Gesellschaft, Hamburg

  12 DKV Deutsche Krankenversicherungs-AG, Köln

  13 DKW, Düsseldorf

  14 Facit GmbH, Düsseldorf

  15 Farbenfabriken Bayer AG, Leverkusen

  16 Ford, Köln

  17 GEG Grosseinkaufsgenossenschaft Deutscher Konsumgenossenschaften, Kamen

  18 Gehrung & Neiweiser, Bielefeld

  19 Goetzewerke, Friedrich Goetze AG, Burscheid

  20 Grünzweig & Hartmann AG, Ludwigshafen

  21 Hoesch AG, Westfalenhütte, Dortmund

  22 Helmut Horten GmbH, Düsseldorf

  23 IBM, Sindelfingen

  24 Innungskrankenkasse, Krefeld

  25 Kaufhalle GmbH, Köln

26 Klöckner-Humboldt-Deutz AG, Köln-Deutz
27 Krafft Velveta, Frankfurt am Main
28 Fried. Krupp, Maschinen- und Stahlbau, Rheinhausen
29 Leipziger Verein Barmenia, Wuppertal-Barmen
30 Emil Lux, Remscheid
31 Mannesmann-Export-GmbH, Düsseldorf
32 Mannheimer Versicherungsgesellschaft
33 Möller-Werke, Brackwede
34 Nino GmbH & Co., Nordhorn
35 Orenstein-Koppel und Lübecker Maschinenbau AG, Dortmund
36 Osram GmbH, München
37 B. Rawe & Co., Nordhorn
38 Schualbach, Braunschweig
39 Siemag Feinmechanische Werke GmbH, Eiserfeld
40 Siempelkamp & Co., Maschinenfabrik, Krefeld
41 Spar, Duisburg
42 Staatsanwaltschaft, Darmstadt
43 Stadtwerke, Lübeck
44 Thyssen Röhrenwerke AG, Düsseldorf
45 Unilever, Hamburg
46 Verlag Buch und Ton, Gütersloh
47 Volkswagenwerk, Wolfsburg
48 Vorwerk & Co., Wuppertal/Bannen (Abt. Datenverarbeitung)
49 Westfalia Separator, Oelde
50 Wohnungsbaukasse, Hamburg
51 Zürich-Hochhaus, Frankfurt am Main

At present about 90 open-plan offices set up in West Germany can be called modern and functional. Effective economy in terms of increased output and decreased costs can, however, be established in only a few of these concerns. The reason for this is that the opportunities offered by the open-plan office for lowering costs per unit of output are not being consistently grasped. The open-plan office cannot be held responsible for failure to make full use of its output advantages*.

The open-plan office is to be found in almost any branch of business

* In just the same way, one cannot make EDP installations responsible for the fact that according to American and German researches, in more than 60 per cent of cases, introduction of EDP has not resulted in a real reduction of costs per unit of output. The efficiency advantages offered by both EDP plants and open-plan offices must be furthered by managerial decisions on staff, material and capital costs, in order to show themselves in the output/costs ratio.

or administration. Design and drawing offices (technical offices) are open plan in at least 80 per cent of cases, generally without textile floor coverings or sound-absorbing ceiling and wall linings. They are also without many of the features mentioned in Section 1.2, because drawing boards have a certain partitioning function and with good organization the working conditions in this case are better than in normal office departments. Even the control desks and card-punching and checking sections of data processing departments, which emit considerable noise, are successfully incorporated in open-plan offices in many cases, although they must be effectively shut off from other office departments by screens and other sound-absorbing measures [14]. Even the directors of large undertakings can be found in open-plan offices, e.g. Buch und Ton Verlag (Gütersloh), Mannheimer Versicherung (Mannheim), Nino (Nordhorn) and Orenstein (Dortmund). Qualified secretaries can also be accommodated in an open-plan office, even if their bosses have their own rooms. In the USA particularly it is usual for the secretary to occupy an open workplace directly in front of the door of the head of the department.

One can find in the open-plan office quite different and unconnected functions, e.g. sales, accounts, legal and income tax, within the same plane. Several open-plan designs have recently proved that even functions totally removed from one another can be catered for in a common open-plan office*. In this connection even isolated single or double workplaces, which are considered by many authors to have a typically closed-plan function [1, p 25], e.g. two secretaries or two assistants exchanging reciprocal information, can be incorporated in an open-plan office next to other alien functions. Even senior employees and persons working on their own can find an appropriate workplace in an open-plan office. In the last-mentioned cases, however, the closed-plan solution may be just as advantageous as the open plan, if not more so.

* The Petzold Study Group takes a different view and considers that in any case, groups of more than 80 workers would seldom be found in one homogenous sphere of function [1, pp 23 and 25].

Chapter 2

The organization of the open-plan office

The guiding principles for the technical organization of an open-plan office are both specific, depending upon the individual administrative and working situation, and also general and function-related. The basic criteria enable one to ascertain the problem to be solved in every case so that the desired function is fulfilled. The outcome of organizational re-thinking should be concerned with: division into departments, planning of departments, new work cycles and resultant workplace layout, choice and utilization of fixed and movable fittings, nature and extent of the work product and the staff to be allocated in number, qualifications and working procedures. These individual data of optimum work organization constitute the concrete principles on which to base the equipping of the open-plan office*. From the individual work situation are derived particular needs as regards decoration, extent of sound-proofing devices, degree of lighting, etc. Such components which are individual to each concern, cannot be generalized about and require particular organization at the planning stage in every case.

Over and above this there are general guidelines for the fitting out of open-plan offices.

2.1 Sound-proofing

An American life assurance company [2, 16, 17, 18] has carried out extensive organizational and medically approved tests in open-plan offices equipped with optimum sound-proofing devices and found the following improvements over work performed in non-sound-proofed open-plan offices:

Increase in output of office employees	8·8 per cent
Reduction of errors by shorthand-typists	29 per cent
Reduction of errors by comptometer operators	52·5 per cent
Decline in illness (absenteeism)	37·5 per cent
Decline in staff turnover	47 per cent

* See also [15, p 34] for the planning of industrial manufacturing buildings.

A noise level of up to 60 phon is considered unharmful. Noise above 65 phon sets off physical reactions (constriction of blood vessels). A noise level above 90 phon can begin to cause permanent organic damage. If possible, office work should not be subjected to a higher noise level than 55 phon. According to Gottschalk [19, p 104 *et seq.*] for work requiring:

Continuous mental concentration	25–45 phon is desirable
Medium concentration	50–60 phon is tolerable

In the Buch und Ton publishing house (Gütersloh) the following values were found after acquisition of an open-plan office:

Over-all average in the office	49–50 phon
Business department	30–35 phon
Machine departments	65 phon

With the same type, number and intensity of sources of noise, the open-plan office always gives lower noise levels than the closed-plan office. Scientific measurements made under absolutely equal noise-source conditions, e.g. in the Mannheimer Versicherung (Mannheim), have clearly proved this. In particular the open-plan office shows fewer contrasts than the closed-plan office.

In a technically well sound-proofed open-plan office there is a:

Comprehension radius of	3·50 m
Hearing radius of	·6·00 m

From a distance of 6·5 m individual sounds are no longer perceived because they mingle in a general level of noise. In the open-plan office noise diffuses, the sound waves break on numerous fittings and screens before they meet solid walls. In the closed-plan office the reflection of sound is several times greater because of the closely facing walls. In the open-plan office arhythmic sounds are diminished and noise peaks lessened with a resultant uniformly levelled noise picture. Although the uniform noise level in the open-plan office is, objectively speaking, a few degrees higher than the arithmetic average noise in the closed-plan office, this higher level is felt to be lower or at least less disturbing because it does not contain jarring noise peaks.

The aim of sound-proofing measures in the open-plan office is by no means the complete elimination of noise. Helmut Sopp, an industrial psychologist, said at a DIB Conference in Frankfurt am Main (1963): 'Disturbances are necessary: office noise is work in progress and the war cry has always been necessary to valiant action.' An underoccupied open-plan office with a low noise level of about 10 phon is far from ideal. A certain measure of noise constitutes a continuous stimulus, particularly for monotonous routine tasks.

The following sound-proofing measures should be applied in the open-plan office:

1 INSULATION FROM OUTSIDE SOUND Thermopane glazing or double-glazing.

2 FLOOR COVERING Cork linoleum or cork parquet; deep pile fitted carpet.

3 SPATIAL SOUND-PROOFING Lining of ceilings, walls and cup-board backs with sound-absorbing material, e.g. acoustic panels, of wood fibre, plaster, aluminium, mineral fibre, etc.

4 SCREENS Lining with textile fabric, foam material or sound-deadening plastic material.

5 FURNITURE Provided with rubber paddings.

6 MACHINES Silenced, covered with hoods; telephone bells set to soft ring or equipped with buzzer; optical instead of acoustic calling system.

7 INSULATION OF NOISE SOURCES Unavoidable noise generators should be concentrated in certain zones and effectively shut off from the other work groups by screens.

One of the most significant and most disturbing sources of noise is that made by people. There is only one remedy: to speak softly.

The sum total of all sound-proofing measures costs approximately 120–130 DM per square metre of office floor space, i.e. about 1,250 DM per office workplace [19, p 125]. Assuming a useful life of only ten years, the proportionate periodic cost per workplace inclusive of interest amounts to approximately 165 DM per year ≈ 14 DM per month = 1·2 per cent of the average staff costs of an office workplace*.

* The Petzold Study Group [1, p 3] considers that sound-absorbing measures are more expensive in open-plan offices than in conventional offices. This is not true. The provision of identical sound-absorbing ceilings, walls and floor coverings is cheaper

It must be said in favour of textile or synthetic fibre carpeting that it stands up to the effects of high-heeled shoes more successfully than PVC flooring. In addition female staff can be advised to wear shoes without stiletto heels in the office, as they are kinder to flooring, e.g. in the Munich chemical factory of Von der Heyden AG.

2.2 Lighting

Uniform distribution of light fittings over the entire extent of the ceiling gives the most favourable lighting conditions. There is then minimum reflection and maximum independence between the lighting system and a flexible workplace arrangement, every part of the office being uniformly illuminated on all sides. The light should be non-glaring and free of reflection and shadow, this being achieved either through the design of the light fittings or by a built-in diffusing grid. The light fittings should be mounted in the ceiling and project slightly downwards therefrom [20, p 140].

Opinions as to the necessary and optimum light intensity are many and varied. For example:

Henn (1955) [in 15, p 73] states	150 lx for office work
	300 lx for drawing work
Rebske (1968) [in 2, p 129] states	250 lx for office work
	250–600 lx for technical drawing offices

Recently there has been a tendency towards higher intensities. Various authors have specified:

For office work	400–600 lx (**Schnelle**)
	740 lx (**Reznik**)
	500–600 lx (**Zobel**)
For drawing work	500–1,000 lx

over large areas in the open-plan office than for the same floor area in closed-plan offices. If the authors mean that in the open-plan office sound-proofing is essential, whilst in the small multi-person office it is not, and therefore the capital outlay for open-plan offices is greater, they are correct as far as outlay on sound-proofing measures is concerned, but not in respect of the total capital expenditure on internal insulation, more especially the day-to-day running costs of the open-plan office. This has been proved by many office buildings that have been constructed.

Hess found in the USA in 1961 [14, p 45] (at the Connecticut Life Insurance Company, Bloomfield, USA) an intensity of 590 lx.

The general technical opinion today is that light intensities of below 500 lx are no longer adequate. Gottschalk [19, p 149] recommends:

For office work   500–750 lx
For drawing work   750–1,000 lx

The lighting consultancy service of Osram (Munich) recommends 1,300 lx for office premises generally. In the USA today the usual values are:

For normal office premises   700–1,000 lx
For drawing offices   1,000–2,000 lx

Technical investigations [21] into lighting have found increased fatigue and diminished performance above 1,000 lx. A definite increase in output is found when rising from 300 to 500 lx as shown in Table 2.1.

Table 2.1

Light intensity, lx	Work performance rating	
	Germany	*USA*
300	100	100
500	100·4	104·6
750	101·3	106·1
1,000	101·8	106·9

According to these findings Germans apparently are not stimulated by lighting to the same extent as Americans.

Although a higher degree of illumination would generally appear to be necessary for drawing work than for normal office work, individual workplace lighting is still not recommended. General lighting is to be preferred to individual lighting in every case (in the closed-plan as well as the open-plan office).

2.3 Colour

Colour in a room is an aesthetic element and therefore of considerable importance for personal well-being. It is also a considerable influence within the sphere of measures aimed at increasing work motivation and raising efficiency.

Since Goethe at least, and right up to the present time, people have been investigating the psychological effects of colour, and a detailed account is therefore superfluous [22]. To give a general outline:

WARM COLOURS bring things nearer and increase the feeling of warmth.

COLD COLOURS (blue, grey, violet) make a room larger and suggest coolness.

DARK ROOMS require bright colours.

Well accepted colours for offices following these precepts are:

WALLS Green/yellow, beige.

WINDOW WALLS Always light, white best.

FLOORS Dark so as not to show dirt (olive green, grey, anthracite, brown). When stimulating colours are required and there is not much dirt: gold shades.

PILLARS/POSTS Contrast colours, e.g. markedly light or markedly dark.

BLINDS Light, e.g. light grey or light green.

Generally speaking a single main colour should predominate in an office. One or two secondary colours may support the main colour [23, p 78]. Bright, light-reflecting, but nevertheless warm tones are to be preferred as main colours, viz:

UNRESTFUL WORK Blue, violet, olive green, grey, little contrast.

MONOTONOUS WORK Yellow, red, marked light-dark contrasts.

NOISY ROOMS Light or olive green, blue-yellow, light colours.

DEALINGS WITH THE PUBLIC Standing, blue; sitting, orange [in 2, p 119 et seq.].

Rest rooms should have restful, warm colours.

2.4 Air-conditioning

Air-conditioning is advisable and economic both for the open- and the closed-plan office. Reductions in efficiency through extreme fluctuations in temperature, through space over-heating or under-cooling, as well as the resultant man-hours lost through sickness, have in the author's experience sometimes been as much as 80 per cent in some cases. Such losses are avoided by air-conditioning. On average one can count on a permanent rise in output of at least 6 per cent as a result of air-conditioning. The figure for any one concern must be accurately determined individually, because it depends on the local temperature and climatic conditions and on the general state of health of the personnel.

In comparisons of types of offices, the costs of air-conditioning plants are often quoted as one disadvantage of open-plan offices. This is unfair. Air-conditioning plants are just as advantageous and advisable in closed-plan offices, where they also increase output. Although they constitute a very desirable feature of an open-plan office, they are by no means a *sine qua non* thereof. Apart from official regulations governing the compulsory installation of air-conditioning plants in tall buildings, and local conditions making window ventilation impossible in particularly windy areas, open-plan offices can be built without any air-conditioning. It is quite remarkable that in South Africa, which is such a hot country, modern office buildings, even high blocks containing open-plan offices, are constructed without air-conditioning plants, and yet office work is still performed efficiently and productively. Nevertheless, air-conditioning of offices must still be considered the optimum solution.

An air-conditioning plant regulates temperature, humidity, oxygen content, air cleanliness and circulation. Whereas window ventilation lets dust and street noise into the office and draughts hinder work and have an adverse effect on workers' health, air conditioning eliminates these external influences. Colds and chills (through draughts) are reduced and other nuisances disappear. Biological tests of air samples, e.g. in the firm of Buch und Ton (Gütersloh), have revealed a smaller proportion of bacteria in air-conditioned than in non-air-conditioned offices. An electroconditioning plant avoids fatigue phenomena by automatic maintenance of a natural ion content in the office atmosphere.

Differing values are given for optimum humidity:

1 HENN 40–60 per cent relative humidity.
2 RIMPL In summer at 22°C temperature, 70 per cent relative humidity and in winter at 20°C temperature, 35–70 per cent relative humidity.

DIN Standard 4701 requires an average temperature of 20°C in the office. Rimpl [23] allows 22°C in summer, 20°C in winter. Gottschalk

25

[19] also quotes 20–22°C. Joerdicke [20, p 117] states that the difference between wall and air temperature should not exceed 1–2 degC, which is not consistent with the above-mentioned temperature limits.

Air movement in an air-conditioning plant may be up to 0·2 m/sec. Higher circulating speeds produce draughts, which again constitute a source of colds, or at least (if the plant is installed in the window frame) necessitate the construction of a space-consuming partition about 60 cm from the window wall and 1·20 m high, in order to direct the air current vertically upwards. It cannot be denied that in many office buildings the air-conditioning plant has created considerable difficulties, at least during a running-in period of up to two years. In particular draughts have had harmful effects, inducing the personnel to set up their workplaces away from the source of draught with consequent large floor space losses, causing colds and chills and making staff wrap up in the most bizarre manner while working. As upsetting and unpleasant as these phenomena may be, objectively they must be considered as the teething troubles of a new technique, which will have its problems solved within a few years.

The installation of an air-conditioning plant precludes the exclusive use of desks with sub-structures standing solidly on the floor, as well as floor-to-ceiling walls. Furniture must have broom clearance, and sectional walls and partitions must be open top and bottom, to allow free or directed circulation of air.

The absolute capital outlay for a technically highly developed air-conditioning plant is considerable. According to Gottschalk [19, p 146]* it may be as high as 13 to 15 per cent of the total building costs. On an average one can reckon about 2,000 DM air-conditioning outlay per office workplace. Assuming a period of use of 30 years this equals (approximately):

For depreciation and interest	120 DM per year
Plus operating costs for maintenance, repair, electricity	180 DM per year
Total	300 DM per year†
	=25 DM per month
	=2·5% of staff costs

* See also [24]. The chief administrative department of Barmenia (Wuppertal) spent for example 15 per cent of the total building costs of a new administration building on the air-conditioning plant.

† Zeh gives the annual costs as 320 DM per workplace [25].

If, on the other hand, an increase in output of 6 per cent is achieved, an air-conditioning plant is clearly economic. It breaks even if an additional net rise in productivity of 3·5 per cent is achieved.

2.5 Furniture

The open-plan office presupposes certain conditions of furniture design. The air-conditioning aspect requires a clear floor and the avoidance of certain large, solid furniture units, in order to ensure the necessary circulation of air. The acoustic aspect favours the widespread abandonment of large smooth surfaces as in the ideal form of unit-furniture. Fixed, solid sub-structures of desks and smooth, extended cupboard surfaces cause excessive sound reflection and increase the noise level. Since about 1960, the aesthetic aspect, which is in any case very changeable, calls for office furniture which is pleasant to look at and rests on slim steel legs without solid fixed sub- or super-structures. The emphasis is on attractiveness rather than solidity. How far these aspects can be taken into account when they conflict with others unrelated to spatial design, such as adaptation to the work product and work technique, confidential or prestige considerations, and so on, can only be decided in each case. Although to ignore or fail to take these aspects fully into account brings certain disadvantages, these are less significant than non-observance of the criteria for fitting out an open-plan office mentioned in Sections 2.1–2.4.

There are three possible forms of workplace arrangement in the open-plan office:

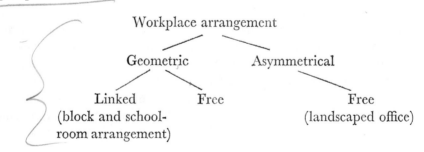

Workplace arrangement

Geometric   Asymmetrical

Linked   Free   Free
(block and school-   (landscaped office)
room arrangement)

Effective use: 100 per cent   80–85 per cent   67–73 per cent

Geometric arrangement is restricted exclusively to a parallel or rectangular alignment of the places, and favours either a layout linked to one direction or a rectangular form which may be more or less free according to the requirements of the situation. On the other hand, the asymmetrical layout is on the free design principle, with key positions, subsidiary positions, work flow, sequential work stages and circular and other arrangements which, whilst dynamically orientated on the basis of functional continuity, follow aesthetic principles. The geometric arrangement occupies the smallest floor space, can be overseen very easily and facilitates the installation of fixed, mechanical stationery-transporting devices (conveyor belts). On the debit side it gives rather the impression of serried army ranks. The asymmetric arrangement occupies much more floor space and is less ordered for overseeing purposes, but it gives the office employee a freer feeling of spaciousness, allows the development of personality and, assisted by plants and flexible arrangements of screens and cupboards, gives a more pleasant impression of an office landscape. Mixed forms are also conceivable, their combination of a linked and free geometric arrangement with asymmetrically disposed workplaces giving space utilization values somewhere between the above extremes, e.g. C. F. Boehringer Söhne (Mannheim), 91 per cent.

Most open-plan offices are designed with geometric workplace arrangement because of the smaller space requirement, and this is also the predominant layout in closed-plan offices.

School-room and block formations occupy the same amount of space but have differing advantages and disadvantages. The block formation facilitates team work and work flow procedures within the group and requires fewer telephone connections. However, the noise and disturbance factors are so great that this type of layout has to be rejected in the majority of cases. The school-room arrangement, on the other hand, causes less distraction, much less loss of time and allows concentrated and isolated work. These advantages are likewise offered by the free geometric and the free asymmetrical formation, but they offer in addition, opportunities for team work without the disadvantages of the block arrangement. All three workplace layouts are justified and offer specific advantages, which can be utilized individually or in combination in the particular case being planned*. An important planning

* Personal attitudes of various authors to the asymmetric formation range from forceful disapproval to enthusiastic approbation. For example, Otto Ladner calls it a 'maze' and says that in a factory it 'would scarcely occur to anyone to install the machines or conveyor belts from an artistic standpoint, or even to leave it to the workers to decide how they wish to arrange their machines' [26]; or Manfred Sack:

feature in workplace arrangement is the provision of space for office furniture. One calculates* either:

1 NET AREA PER WORKPLACE Area requirement without aisles determined per workplace type,

or:

2 GROSS AREA PER WORKPLACE Average area requirement per workplace including proportionate access area and general furniture of the department.

For rough preliminary plans the gross area is sufficient; for detailed area distribution plans, drawn to scale, directly before occupation of a new open-plan office, the net area should be calculated.

Screens in the open-plan office may be visual or acoustic, or serve for grouping and room-dividing. Although they reduce visibility, which is one of the advantages of the open-plan office, they nevertheless are an indispensable feature thereof. The number of screens has to be adapted to the requirements of individual concerns. In the average case of a normal mixture of general and management departments, there is one screen to three employees. With a screen height of 1·40 or 1·60 m one can still see over them comfortably from a standing position. They do not need to be higher than 1·80 m. The width can be adapted to the desk top dimensions or standardized (1·56 m, 1·60 m, 1·70 m). Semi-circular screens are conceivable for working groups or as sound booths. Rectangular screens can be used both for geometric and asymmetrical workplace layouts including circular arrangements, with appropriate sectioning.

Plant and flower tubs for green plants should be placed freely about the room and along the aisles. This gives a feeling of spaciousness and makes the working atmosphere more pleasant, and also brings a natural element into the office world, giving the general impression of an office landscape. Moreover, specifically selected plants contribute to air purification, because they absorb and convert carbon dioxide. Watering and general care of flowers and plants can either be left to the staff in the direct vicinity or allocated to a central gardener.

If one includes in the cost of fitting out an open-plan office workplace —desk and chairs, additional furniture, partitioning elements, a

'The empty open space must become an office landscape—one might consider the metaphor not of a plantation, but of a natural although ordered park' [27].

* Detailed figures are given in Appendix 2 and [1, p 37 *et seq.*].

proportion for files and conferences and for a rest room, cloakroom and curtains—but not air-conditioning, lighting, flooring and ceiling—the following average values (in DM per workplace) are obtained, according to Gottschalk [19, p 202]:

Clerical staff	1,100
Professional and technical assistants	1,350
Shorthand-typist/clerks	1,400
Group supervisors	1,800
Department heads	3,900

The consumption of sandwiches and other food is just as undesirable in the open-plan office as in the closed office, and in order to prevent tea or coffee breaks having a disturbing influence, those concerned should have their break in the rest room. Recently 'free break organization' has been introduced into most concerns, to great advantage. The time, frequency and length of breaks is left to the employee, thus enabling him to organize his breaks according to his own biological working rhythm as well as to the individual workplace requirements [19, p 80]. A rest room should be provided on each floor. One should calculate 0·7 m² rest room area per 10 m² of effective office area (=per office workplace). The cloakroom can be included in this if the cloakroom lockers are used to demarcate the rest room [3]. The rest room may be located in a preferred corner with an outside view, but it is more rational to place it at the technical nucleus, because it requires a water supply, and the break is often associated with the use of the toilet facilities of the core. Rest room and toilets should if possible be not further than about 100 m from the workplace [14, p 91].

Piped music can increase output both in open-plan and closed-plan offices. It is permissible for it to increase the level of work noise by a few phon, and it thereby exerts a noise-levelling function at the same time. The type of music to be relayed—dance music, marches, pop, jazz, light music, classical music—is dependent on numerous factors and must be related to the individual concern or even the individual department, depending on the sex, average age, work activities, social status, general atmosphere, working environment, etc. It is a known fact that music should not be relayed the whole day, but only during certain potentially fatiguing periods [14, p 51]. There are so far in Germany few firms having significant music provision in offices, e.g. Braun AG (Frankfurt am Main) and Neuhaus (Witten).

Chapter 3

Profitability of the open-plan office

Previously it has not been usual and has even been thought impossible to draw up profitability figures for office buildings. However, the widespread scepticism as to the desirability of the open-plan office compels one to look at the problem from an exact, mathematical standpoint. The profitability of the open-plan office can be worked out from the formula:

$$\frac{\text{Productivity of the open-plan office}}{\text{Expenditure on the open-plan office}} = \frac{\text{Profitability of}}{\text{the open-plan office}}$$

If the outputs in the open-plan and the closed-plan offices were identical, the profitability could be worked out solely from the costs formula:

$$\frac{\text{Costs of the closed-plan office}}{\text{Costs of the open-plan office}} = \frac{\text{Profitability of}}{\text{the open-plan office}}$$

If the costs of both types of office were identical, one would only have to compare the productivity figures. However, experience has shown that neither the productivity nor the costs of closed- and open-plan offices are identical. Although there are many exact although conflicting figures available for the costs of an open-plan office, the output side has so far remained largely uninvestigated.

In the costs of open-plan office premises one has to distinguish:

Capital costs (fixed costs).
Depreciation, e.g. 1–2 per cent.
Rent.
Interest, e.g. 6 per cent.
Repairs.
Insurances.
Ground rent or land tax.
Rates and taxes for water supply, drainage, refuse removal, street cleaning, chimney cleaning, window cleaning, etc.
Security.

Operating costs (variable costs).
Heating.
Air-conditioning.
Electricity.
Cleaning.
Wages for caretaker, service of technical installations, maintenance.
Conversions.

As an example of such a calculation an old building with an extension with closed-plan offices has been chosen [1, pp 114–15], the costs of which are given in Table 3.1. The figures for the costs of a building site

Table 3.1

Nature of costs	DM/m² in	
	Month	Year
Capital costs		
Depreciation, rent, interest	1·92	23·04
Repairs, insurances, rates, taxes, security	1·14	13·68
Total	3·06	36·72
Operating costs		
Heating, electricity (without air-conditioning)	0·72	8·64
Cleaning	1·06	12·72
Maintenance of building	0·42	5·04
Total	2·20	26·40
Total costs	5·26	63·12

and for building costs are given in Standards Leaflets DIN 276 and 277 published by the Technical Standards (Building) Department of the German Standards Institute*.

The actual open-plan office premises do not have any output, they merely make possible the output of the personnel working in them. When considering the office premises in isolation, it is impossible to ascribe a part of the personnel output to the environmental factors of the premises and part to personal or other factors. Only with absolutely

* English equivalents are available from the London Group of Building Centres, London, Manchester and Cambridge. London address: 26 Store Street, London WC1.

identical conditions of staff, work and means can one compare productivity in two or more different types of office and attribute the
difference in productivity to the conditions of the respective premises.
In this sense, by productivity of the open-plan office is meant the
difference in the personnel output evaluated in an open-plan office
compared with that in the closed-plan office. One then has merely to
relate the output difference to the costs difference:

$$\frac{\text{Productivity difference of open-plan office}}{\text{Expenditure difference of open-plan office}} = \frac{\text{Profitability of}}{\text{open-plan office}}$$

Even if the productivity in the open-plan office were less than in the
closed-plan office, the open-plan office could be economic because of
lower costs. Even if the total costs of the open-plan office were higher
than those of the closed-plan office, the open-plan office could be
economic through additional productivity compensating the negative
costs, difference. Since, however—as will be shown in the following
section—both higher productivity and lower costs are the result in
optimally designed open-plan offices, the open-plan office is economic
from both aspects. One is therefore also justified in considering profitability on the costs side and the output side separately, because a
positive result on one side cannot be cancelled by a negative result on
the other. As so far it has not been possible scientifically to measure
the productivity of office work in monetary terms, the above profitability formula cannot be calculated and stated monetarily. One has
therefore to be satisfied with measuring productivity in units of
quantity. The calculation of profitability is thereby simplified into
several profitability comparisons with corresponding units of measurement in each case. In these the costs or output factors of open-plan and
closed-plan offices are contrasted.

3.1 Comparison of building expenditure

The capital investment (wrongly referred to in common parlance as
'building costs') for an office building includes the entire expenditure
on planning including architects' fees and costs of below- and above-
ground building including exacavation, foundations, basement, shell
costs, the entire installation and inside decoration, sanitary and
electrical fitting, windows, lighting, ceiling construction, flooring

and paintwork, air-conditioning plants, but excluding the cost of the site, excluding movable fittings and excluding external extensions, such as car-parks, garages, swimming pools and sports grounds but including canteen and kitchens. This definition (which is not an entirely logical one) is used today by architects, building departments of firms and managements when compiling building expenditure figures. This undoubtedly makes comparison difficult in many cases, because, for example, not all office blocks are equipped with an air-conditioning plant and canteen. Additionally there is the not inconsiderable difficulty of obtaining an exact mathematical calculation of the effective capital investment, which not uncommonly, is stated by the building department, outside architects and internal organizer and management as four distinct figures, varying by as much as 15 per cent, for the same new building. Differing definitions and methods of calculation, over-emphasis of certain aspects to suit a particular public policy, and varying degrees of enjoyment of publicity in the sphere of prestige spending (in which office blocks may be at least partly included), all render it very difficult to make generally valid pronouncements on capital building expenditure. However, these uncertainty factors do not affect open-plan constructions solely, they occur in the same ratio with regard to new buildings for both closed-plan and open-plan offices. For this reason and because these factors do not seem to weigh more heavily on either the positive or the negative side, one may justifiably (despite reservations) ascribe at least a relative authenticity to the many statements as to capital expenditure on building.

The decisive question is: Does the open-plan office require greater building outlay than the closed plan?

The Petzold Study Group states [1, p 23 *et seq.*] that open-plan offices entail additional expenditure, or at least do not offer any reduction in building costs, because of:

1 Asymmetrical arrangement of workplaces (high workspace requirements).
2 Erection of screens, shelving, plant tubs (higher space requirements).
3 Greater span of ceiling construction.
4 Greater storey height (instead of 3·25 m in air-conditioned closed-plan offices—4 to 4·50 m) hence up to 30 per cent greater building volume.
5 Full air-conditioning with up to 25 per cent higher building costs.

6 Acoustic provision—coffered and panelled ceilings, carpeted floors and screens.

This statement conflicts, however, with the publication by the same Schmalenbach-Gesellschaft [12, p 106 *et seq.*] of the capital expenditure comparison (price basis 1962) shown in Table 3.2. Although this table

Table 3.2

Mean capital expenditure per		Building outlay, DM	
		Closed-plan	Open-plan
1–9 storeys	Place	7,500–17,000	—
10–13 storeys	Place	15,000–21,000	—
High buildings, air-conditioned	Place	20,000–25,000	—
Low buildings, air-conditioned	Place	—	11,000–20,000

is based on a relatively small number of open-plan office buildings, it shows the definite superiority of the open-plan office as regards building outlay.

Meanwhile there have been numerous individual statements and figures proving that the open-plan office requires a smaller capital outlay. Joedicke [20, p 13] has found generally lower building expenditure in open-plan offices compared with closed-plan ones. *Maschine und Manager* [28] states for so-called 'cellular construction' (closed-plan offices) 10,000–25,000 DM capital outlay, for the open-plan office a maximum of 15,000 DM per workplace

Barmenia-Versicherung (Wuppertal) have ascertained from a costs comparison that a new administrative building of open-plan design is approximately 30 per cent cheaper than a corresponding new closed-plan building. Helmut Horten (Düsseldorf) have saved 20 per cent by constructing their new Am Seestern block as open-plan offices. Mannheimer Versicherung (Mannheim) would have had to pay out 10·2 million DM for closed-plan offices instead of 7·8 million DM for the open-plan building. According to Ladner [29, p 137], Mannheimer Versicherung were able to make a 20 per cent saving in area. In two other insurance companies with open-plan offices a saving of 15 per cent on building costs compared with closed-plan solutions has been achieved.

To effect a comparison of capital outlay for open-plan and closed-plan designs, one can draw on the area requirement per workplace, the effective office area as a percentage of the total area, and the expenditure per square metre or cubic metre of workplace. The expressions 'effective area' and 'office area' first need to be clarified:

1 Schmalenbach-Gesellschaft [12, pp 8 and 18] distinguish:
General rooms (telephone switchboard, filing department, reprographic rooms, canteen, showroom, workshops)
+ Office areas
= Effective area
+ Subsidiary areas (vestibules, stairs, lifts, w.c., technical installations)
= Total area

Building departments and organization departments of individual firms, on the other hand, have given different definitions, e.g.:

2 Buch und Ton (Gütersloh):
Office area (without rest rooms and technical installations)
+ Subsidiary areas (cloakrooms, forms depository)
+ Staircases, toilets, rest rooms
= Total area
3 Rheinstahl (Essen):
Effective area (offices, subsidiary areas, technical rooms)
+ Traffic area
= Total area
4 Fried. Krupp Maschinen- und Stahlbau (Rheinhausen):
Effective area
+ Technical area
= Total area

In the following remarks use of the term 'effective area' is based on the Schmalenbach-Gesellschaft definition.

In Table 3.3 area and capital expenditure are listed for 25 recently constructed new buildings or conversions with closed-plan or open-plan offices. From this comparison of a number of administrative buildings, which can be enlarged by further examples showing the same tendency, the following clear conclusions can be drawn:

1 Open-plan buildings occupy less area per workplace than closed-plan buildings.

2 Open-plan buildings have a proportionally greater effective office area than closed-plan buildings.

3 Open-plan buildings tie up less capital per workplace and cubic metre than closed-plan buildings.

4 Low buildings have a greater effective office area, and lower area and outlay requirement per workplace than high buildings.

This comparison of capital expenditure for open- and closed-plan offices thus comes out clearly in favour of the open-plan office.

3.2 Comparison of maintenance costs

As depreciation, rent or interest are given as capital expenditure figures, a renewed profitability comparison of capital costs is unnecessary. The other fixed costs—repairs, insurances, land tax or ground rent, rates and taxes, security—are also largely proportional to the capital expenditure and can therefore be disregarded in a profitability comparison.

Maintenance costs (upkeep costs, current running costs) take a different course. These mainly include the current costs of air-conditioning, heating and ventilation, water and electricity supply, wages, cleaning of floors and windows.

Individual inquiries in various concerns have shown lower total upkeep costs in open-plan offices than in closed-plan offices. Thus Rodius [30] has found the following annual upkeep costs for two different office buildings of Nino GmbH (Nordhorn):

Open-plan building (with air-conditioning)   DM 25·40/m²
Closed-plan building (without air-conditioning) DM 36·50/m²

Barmenia (Wuppertal) have found 18 per cent lower total maintenance costs (including air-conditioning) in an open-plan office compared with that in closed-plan offices (without air-conditioning).

Of particular interest in this connection are floor cleaning costs. An optimally designed open-plan office is best carpeted in synthetic fibre (Perlon, Dralon, or the like) for reasons of sound-absorption, general environment, and ease and economy of cleaning. Table 3·4 shows floor cleaning costs that have been derived from experiences in a large number of concerns. In spite of the much higher price of fitted carpet, the very favourable difference in cleaning costs is far greater than the difference in depreciation. Numerous individual findings with partially

Table 3.3

Office type C = closed-plan O = open-plan	Building type H = high L = low	Firm	Place	Storey size			Area per workplace, m²			Capital outlay*	
				Built	Area, m²	Employees	Effective office area, m²	Total	Effective area	Office area	per workplace, DM	per m³, DM
C	H	Rheinstahl	Essen	1961			73	16·5	12	8·5	22,000	320
C	H	Telefunken	Berlin	1960			68	19	12	9·8	23,300	233
C+O	H	Nestle	Vevey	1960	2,600	280	39	23	14	8·5	24,000	200
C+O	H	Esso	Antwerpen	1961	1,200		40	33	13	9	28,000	210
C+O	H	Thyssen-Röhrenw.	Düsseldorf	1960	950		66	24	19	16		
C+O	H	Mannesmann-Export	Düsseldorf	1960	550	40	73	20	13·5	11		
C+O	H	Farbenf. Bayer	Leverkusen	1963	1,264	80	56	15	12·5	11	37,000	
C+O	H	Unilever	Hamburg	1962			77	26	11	8	30,440	318
C+O	H	Pirelli	Mailand				53	10·5	9·5	8	27,600	
O	H	Rhein-Neckar AG	Mannheim	1965			46–79	25	11·4	10	25,000	230

38

○	H	Mannheimer Vers.	Mannheim	1960	656	620	75	20	9	8	12,500	170
○	H	BP (Testraum)	Hamburg	1962			92	12·5	12	11	4,000†	250
○	L	Helmut Horten GmbH	Düsseldorf	1962	7,100	700	82	12·6	10	9·8	11,500	148
○	L	NINO GmbH & Co.	Nordhorn	1963	2,150	155	78	15·6	11·5	10·5	11,600	162
○	L	Boehringer & Söhne	Mannheim	1960	1,370	175	89	13	10	7·8	13,500	153
○	L	Fried. Krupp Masch.- u. Stahlbau	Rheinhausen	1962	2,520	275	80	18·5	13·9	9·1		
○	L	Buch und Ton	Gütersloh	1961	2,947	270	90	11	10·9	8	6,000†	
○	L	Friedr. Deckel	München	1963	625		70	16	10	9		
○	L	Osram GmbH	München	1966	2,500		78	14	11·5	10·5		
○	L	KRAVAG	Hamburg	1966			70	16	10	9	20,000	212
○	L	Schmalbach	Braunschweig	1965		125	88	19	10·5	9	16,000	165
○	L	Leipziger Verein Barmenia	Wuppertal	1966	1,500		90	16	9	8·5	18,000	208
○	L	GEG	Kamen	1966			92	13	12	11	24,000	
○	L	Anker Werke	Bielefeld	1964			92	12·5	12	11	3,000†	
○	L	Gehring & Neiweis	Bielefeld	1966	280	26	92	10·8	10	9	5,000†	113†

Missing details were not released for publication. In the case of conflicting data, the more unfavourable value has been given.

* Including auxiliary building costs, air-conditioning plant in open-plan offices, excluding movable fittings.

† Excluding shell costs.

Table 3.4

	PVC linoleum, DM/m²	Synthetic fitted carpet, DM/m²
Price	8·00	48·00
Depreciation (at 10% p.a.) per year	0·80	4·80
Cleaning costs	29·50	12·30
Total costs	30·30	17·10

differing numerical values but with similar ratios confirm this. Hummer [31] states the following annual costs for floor cleaning:

Conventional closed-plan offices with hard floor   DM 13·20/m²
Open-plan offices with textile flooring   DM 6·00/m²

Fried. Krupp (Rheinhausen) found the following annual costs with a Dralon flooring of DLW (Bayer Fibre):

In former closed-plan offices   DM 38·48/m²
In present open-plan office   DM 26·40/m²

because of less expenditure on cleaners and cleaning material.

The large areas in the open-plan office and the absence of doors, walls and corners make for much quicker cleaning compared with the closed-plan office. Thyssen-Röhrenwerke (Düsseldorf) could afford to give the outside cleaning contractor an output target of 90 m²/hr per cleaner, and Thyssen'sche Gas- und Wasserwerke (Duisburg), 100 m²/hr per cleaner. In closed-plan offices cleaning output often reaches only half these areas. A differentiated costs comparison, by Werner Heinrichs (Burscheid), for carpeted and hard floor, for C. F. Boehringer & Söhne (Mannheim) is given in Table 3.5.

The Mannheimer Versicherung (Mannheim) save DM 6,400 in cleaning costs annually by having open-plan offices and carpeted floors.

These numerical values based on areas, which in some cases are very large, take into account the Petzold Study Group's objection [1, p 24] that the operating costs for air-conditioning and lighting rise 'considerably' with room depths of 20–30 m, because:

1 The inner zones must be artificially lighted.
2 The build-up of heat in the inner zones must be additionally remedied by air-conditioning, at least in summer.

Table 3.5 Comparison of costs

Floor carpet, laid in 1960, 3,200 m²	DM	Hard floor in same size office areas	DM
Hourly wages (1·95)	4,212	Hourly wages (1·95)	9,300
10% National Insurance	421	10% National Insurance	930
Internal miscalculation factor (15%)	695	Internal miscalculation factor (15%)	1,534
Work costs	5,328	Work costs	11,764
*Appliances**		*Appliances**	
'Vorwerk-Kobold' vacuum cleaners		'Fakir' floor polishers	
*Current consumption**		*Current consumption**	
Cleaning materials		*Cleaning materials*	
		Wax polish	870
		Steel wool	200
		Turpentine substitute	200
Removal of small stains included in general work costs		Additional work costs for stain removal	950
	5,328		13,984
Annual cleaning costs, per m²	1·66	Annual cleaning costs, per m²	4·37
Difference, per m²			2·71
Difference for the total area, per year			8,656

* Values for appliances and current consumption are substantially equal. They have not been taken into account in the comparison. The cleaning costs are increased by this amount per square metre.

Conversion costs in closed-plan offices must not be underestimated. Functions and departments grow, shrink and alter, new functions arise, old ones disappear. Workplaces have to be constantly regrouped and different allocations of staff made. This means: shifting workplaces, moving furniture, knocking down walls, putting up new walls. An investigation by the author in several concerns showed that about 7 per cent of the staff are affected by moves annually and annual conversion costs in closed-plan blocks amount to DM 2,600 per 100 employees. Osram (Munich) found that conversions in their former old building cost them as much as DM 100,000 per year for 1,000 employees. In open-plan buildings changeovers are, of course, still unavoidable but the cost is far less because there are no walls to pull down and re-erect. Comparable conversion costs in an open-plan building are DM 700 per year per 100 employees.

41

Removal of area boundaries in closed-plan blocks is not only very expensive but often impossible. 'Mistakes once made in concrete and steel, cannot be corrected' [2, p 37].

The costs of air-conditioning are higher than the costs of conventional heating and natural ventilation. Apart from official regulations for high buildings, the air-conditioning plant is justified by more favourable output values (see Section 3.2). Moreover, it is a questionable method to compare air-conditioned open-plan offices with non-air-conditioned closed-plan offices. For all that, if one contrasts the total costs of open-plan maintenance including air-conditioning with the maintenance costs of closed-plan offices, and regards the total maintenance costs of the open-plan office including air-conditioning plant as one unit, the open-plan office incurs lower maintenance costs over-all. It is, therefore, once again clearly superior to the closed-plan office in most office buildings built up to the present. This artificial consideration of the total costs of the object is justified and necessary on technical and organizational grounds. It is also to be recommended for economic reasons, when for certain individual types of cost, higher costs are demonstrated for the open-plan office, without calling its over-all profitability into question.

Zeh [25] has made a costs comparison for an office building with 400 office workplaces and 750 m² of records and stores. The results of the comparison are shown in Table 3.6.

This numerical example does not show to what type of costs and doubtless unusual causes the higher operating costs of the open-plan

Table 3.6

Data	Type of building	Conventional cellular construction, DM	Open-plan storey building, DM	Open-plan low building, DM
	Storeys	10	5	2
Building costs:				
total		8,540,000	6,500,000	5,000,625
per m³		280	250	225
per workplace		21,350	16,250	12,500
Operating costs*				
total per year		199,700	299,700	260,350
per workplace per year		500	750	650

* Cleaning, heating, air-conditioning, electricity.

office are to be attributed. As these numerical values do not correspond to most existing experience, one may be justified in doubting the technical necessity of these high costs. But the chief reason for questioning the validity of these figures is that of the three alternatives mentioned two were not effectively carried out, and the figures given are therefore of a purely theoretical nature. Empirical values carry much more weight. Moreover the total costs of the low open-plan building are, at approximately DM 900 per workplace, below the DM 927 per workplace for cellular construction.

With expertly organized planning and optimum technical design and, at the same time, the most economical procuring of the labour and materials needed to erect a new office building, consideration of total costs results in less expenditure for the open-plan office than for closed-plan offices. Hummer [31] compares a building construction for 410 employees in conventional closed plan and functional open plan (see Table 3.7). With the open-plan office there is a 19·2 per cent saving in capital expenditure and 40 per cent saving in maintenance costs.

Table 3.7*

	Closed plan, DM	Open plan, DM
I Capital expenditure		
1 Building costs	8,325,000	5,816,300
2 Fitting out costs	4,441,000	4,506,000
Total	12,766,000	10,332,300
II Maintenance costs		
1 Depreciation, interest, keeping in repair	444,000	310,200
2 Heating, ventilation (air-conditioning)	52,080	71,000
3 Floor cleaning	163,680	21,300
4 Window and façade cleaning	39,690	12,690
Total	699,450	415,190

* Here the lighting costs are omitted.

Gottschalk [19, p 203] gives a general statement of the annual total costs including fixed costs for building and fittings (see Table 3.8).

According to Gottschalk, therefore—as has already been proved in individual area and costs comparisons of 25 office buildings—the costs of the open-plan low building are more favourable than those of the closed-plan high building. Undoubtedly also—although Gottschalk does not prove this—the costs of the open-plan high building are more favourable than the costs of the closed-plan high building. In normal

Table 3.8 Costs per square metre of total area

DM	Closed-plan offices		Open-plan offices, 2–4 storeys,
	Low building, 3–5 storeys	High building, 14–20 storeys,	
1. *Capital costs*			
Depreciation, interest	36·0	54·0	45·0
2. *Maintenance costs*			
Land and Property tax, insurances	5·3	7·5	6·4
Upkeep and repairs	7·9	12·9	9·5
Outside cleaning, refuse disposal	5·0	10·0	4·0
Total maintenance costs	18·2	30·4	19·9
3. *Operating costs*			
Heating, ventilation, air-conditioning, water	8·8	25·2	18·0
Electricity	6·8	11·0	15·4
Inside cleaning	11·0	11·0	11·0
Total operating costs	26·6	47·2	43·4
Total costs per m² (1 + 2 + 3), DM	80·8	131·6	108·3
Total area (including basement) per work-place, m²	21·0	24·0	17·5
Annual total costs per workplace, DM	1,697·0	3,158·0	1,895·0

buildings of six or more floors—not compared by Gottschalk—the open-plan office is also more profitable. There thus only remains Gottschalk's assertion, neither established empirically nor inferred by deduction, that in low buildings of up to five floors the closed-plan type shows lower annual total costs than the open-plan type. If this statement is true, which seems doubtful in view of the empirical figures submitted by the author in this work (both as regards capital expenditure and maintenance costs) the open-plan low building can nevertheless still be held to be profitable because of its higher productivity. This has to be proved, of course, by monetary evaluation of office outputs and a calculation of the profitability quotient from output and costs.

The comparative figures (empirically substantiated) in Table 3.9 are compiled from the author's experience in more than 1,000 undertakings at home and abroad, of a large number of office building plans that have been executed, and from personal research in almost all the concerns mentioned by name in this book.

These figures show in favour of the open-plan office:

Area	13 per cent more effective area.
	26 per cent saving in total area.
	12 per cent saving in office area.
Capital expenditure	24 per cent saving in capital expenditure.
Costs	Cleaning, 41 per cent saving.
	Conversions, 73 per cent saving per workplace.
	Heating and ventilation, 44 per cent extra cost.
	Operating costs per workplace per year, 27 per cent saving.
Total costs per workplace per year	18 per cent saving.

From the point of view of total costs the open-plan office is more economic than the closed-plan office.

This experience derived from a large number of office buildings does not exclude the possibility that in particular cases the costs situation may favour the closed-plan office. Particularly in low buildings of up to five storeys, the non-air-conditioned closed-plan office may, as has been quoted in two cases, present lower costs under certain circumstances than a comparable open-plan office. Nevertheless, in such a case the output advantages of the open-plan office may outweigh its cost disadvantages. This fact should convince any person about to build of the necessity not only of basing his decisions on general experiences but also on an individual profitability reckoning for the concern in question.

3.3 Comparison of output

In past years the output advantages of open-plan offices have been frequently claimed but seldom proved. Ideas as to the extent of the output advantages are also vague. Hummer [31, p 40] mentions a saving in personnel of 16 per cent through shortening of distances, better communication, better information, better working conditions and

45

Table 3.9 General area and costs comparison

Comparison criteria	Closed plan		Open plan	
	Range	Most frequent value	Range	Most frequent value
Area				
Office-effective area, %	39–73	70	75–92	83
Total area per workplace, m²	16·5–33	21	10·8–25	16
Office area per workplace, m²	8·0–16·0	10·5	8·0–11·0	9·3
Capital expenditure				
Per workplace	22,000–37,000	25,000	11,500–30,440	19,000
(24 per cent capital saving)				
Cleaning costs	PVC floor		Carpeted floor	
Per m² per year, DM	16–38	30	15–30	23
Per workplace per year, DM		630		368
Conversion costs per workplace				
In existing building per year, DM		26		7
From old to new building, DM	46–62	54	42–60	51
Heating, ventilation (air-conditioning)				
Per workplace per year, DM	140–220	180	210–320	260
Operating costs				
Per workplace per year, DM	1,200–2,300	1,650	900–2,100	1,200
Total costs per workplace per year, DM	1,600–3,400	2,250	1,300–3,200	1,840

greater flexibility. Schnelle at an Open-office Conference in Rheinhausen in 1963, published the following results of open-plan offices and air-conditioning in the publishing house of Buch und Ton (Gütersloh):

1 Absenteeism and illness reduced.

2 Quantity of output increased by 20 per cent with the same staff.

The then organization director of Buch und Ton, Dr H. Schmidt, greatly doubted such results, however [32]. The Petzold Study Group of Schmalenbach-Gesellschaft [1, p 113] gives a concrete but non-substantiated figure: 'by combining several split-up offices into a good operating layout' and through 'improved efficiency in office work as a result of more economical management organization in more expediently designed areas' there can be:

1 A 10 per cent saving in employees proportional to the volume of business.

2 A 5 per cent saving in employees not proportional to the volume of business.

These figures may well be correct, but it is debatable whether the second of the above reasons—more economical management organization—is an effect of the new spatial layout or an autonomously acting factor, which although not entirely independent of the room, is an individual force subject to its own costs and output. It would seem causologically more accurate to include in the consideration of profitability of office premises only those output factors arising directly from the spatial arrangement. It then becomes apparent that there is no considerable difference in output between employees proportional to the volume of business and those not proportional thereto as a result of the spatial arrangement, so that the above difference in result seems neither necessary nor justified.

Alsleben [32] carried out an observation of output restricted to two typical office jobs with the results shown in Table 3.10. If one measures

Table 3.10

Type of room	Time, min	
	Adding	Reading
Single room	13	11
Closed plan	21	18
Open plan	16	13·3

the efficiency of staff in the time taken to perform these two jobs and its dependence on the type of room, the single office offers the ability for the greatest concentration and output and the closed-plan or multi-person office the lowest productivity:

Single room	100 per cent
Open-plan office	121 per cent
Multi-person office	163 per cent

According to this the open-plan office has an output advantage of 42 per cent over the group room. These figures, however, do not show how great a proportion of the sum total of office jobs and time consumed in the office is constituted by the functions of 'adding and reading'. It is therefore not possible to infer over-all productivity of the open-plan office from this partial productivity. Numerous other factors influence the output of office employees. One that is well established is the absence of doors and the resultant avoidance of door movements. According to research by the author's consultancy firm, the following values can be expected in closed-plan buildings for 100 persons accommodated in 25 closed offices (four-person rooms):

On an average 11 changes of room per person per day at four movements for door opening and closing

$$= \quad 44 \text{ door movements per person per day}$$
$$= 4,400 \text{ door movements per 100 persons per day}$$
$$= 88,000 \text{ door movements per 100 persons per month.}$$

However instructive and creditable an experiment, it seems extremely problematical to try, as Alsleben did, to infer productivity of the open-plan office from an increase in output in individual jobs considered in isolation. One would also have to compare all the typical office jobs in closed- and open-plan offices, that is, besides adding and reading, typing, telephoning, dictating, taking shorthand, negotiating, deliberating, checking, drawing, etc., about 40–45 different jobs altogether. A general statement cannot be made because these jobs occur in different quantitative and chronological composition in every concern and every department. Moreover, time losses in the office, amounting to between 50 and 90 per cent, on an average about 70 per cent, would not be included, and one can hardly omit such a high proportion of total time consumption from an investigation. Moreover, the effect of the open-plan office on time losses is of particular interest.

For these reasons the author has tried in the following pages to assess the effect of the open-plan office on staff output from the specific environmental conditions of the office. Typical environmental factors of the open-plan office are communications, disturbing actions, noise, air-conditioning, visual range. These influencing factors have been analysed in a large-scale investigation comparing the working conditions in conventional closed-plan offices (multi-person rooms) and optimally designed open-plan offices, by observation, research, measurement and calculation. The investigation relates to a large administrative concern in Rheinland. Chance extreme values have been eliminated. The method used should be universally valid.

3.3.1 Increased output

Increased output by staff in open-plan offices is caused by the following.

3.3.1.1 BETTER COMMUNICATION

1 Absence of door movements: per worker an average of 32 door movements per day @ 7 sec = 640 door movements per month = 74 min/month.

Reduction of wrong calls: of previously about 64 wrong calls per person per month, about 21 are saved @ 0·3 min = 6 min/month. Time saving through better communication: 80 min per worker per month.

3.3.1.2 LESS PRIMARY DISTRACTION*

Primary distraction within one working group in a closed-plan office is caused by telephone calls and visitors.

According to a survey on individual communication by telephone and visits, one office employee has on average in a month:

$$\begin{array}{l} 56 \text{ telephone calls} \\ \underline{47 \text{ visitors (internal and external)}} \\ 103 \text{ primary disturbances} \end{array}$$

In a closed office of four persons each individual disturbance affects four persons. Accordingly each worker is affected monthly by

$$103 \times 4 = 412 \text{ disturbances}$$

The disturbance causes, at least at its beginning and end, a stoppage of output of 4 sec, respectively, i.e. 8 sec altogether. For the duration of the disturbance there is a reduction in output of 18 per cent. The monthly result is shown in Table 3.11. In the open-plan office there is only the disturbance affecting one person (one-quarter of the total amount), i.e. three-quarters of the disturbance time is eliminated: 8,550 sec or 142 min disturbance time per month.

* Primary distraction (centripetal distraction) is a disturbance directed at a single person or working group, e.g. telephone calls, visitors, colleagues, aimed directly at and responded to by the individual and unexpectedly interrupting the occupation of the moment. This primary distraction of the individual directly affected worker is not reduced by the open-plan office, but the associated distraction of the members of the group is.

Secondary distraction (peripheral distraction) is disturbance not directed at certain individuals or working groups but generally perceptible at the periphery of the individual or group, e.g. passing by of persons and visitors foreign to the group, overloud telephoning in another but audible department, etc. Secondary distraction is greater in the open-plan office than in the closed-plan office which is fully screened by side walls.

Table 3.11

No.	Type of disturbance	Duration, sec				Idle disturbance time, sec		Sum of disturbance time, sec/month
		Individual duration	Total	18 per cent thereof		Per disturbance	Total	
224	Telephone calls	50	11,200	2,016		8	1,792	3,808
188	Visitors	180	33,840	6,091		8	1,504	7,595
412							Total	11,403

3.3.1.3. LESS NOISE DISTURBANCE

On the basis of records kept of time distribution, 33 per cent of total office time is spent on noise-creating jobs (telephoning, speaking, machine operating, etc.). With a reduction of noise level from an average of 60 phon during noisy actions in the 4-5 person closed-plan office to an average of 42 phon [34; 19, p 103] in the open-plan office, i.e. a decrease of approximately one-third, impairment of output due to noise is reduced. According to extensive measurements the efficiency curve in relationship to noise intensity is as shown in Fig. 1 and Table 3.12. Accordingly the comparison shown in Table 3.13 can be made.

The ideal nominal value of between 38 and 44 phon can only be

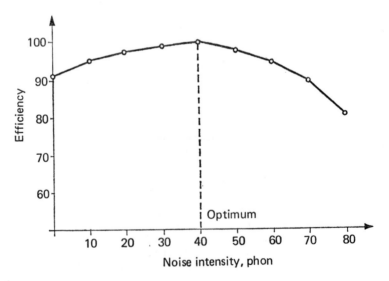

Fig. 1

Table 3.12 Efficiency and noise intensity with repetitive office work

Noise intensity, phon	Efficiency*		
	Effective	Change	
		Individual	Cumulative
0	90·5	−4·5	9·5
10	95	−2·5	5
20	97·5	−1·5	2·5
30	99	−1	1
40	100	0	0
50	98	−2	2
60	94·8	−3·2	5·2
70	89·7	−5·1	10·3
80	80·2	−9·5	19·8

* Excluding creative persons.

Table 3.13

Office type	Noise intensity, phon	Efficiency
Closed plan	60	94·8
Open plan	42	99·6

achieved in an open-plan office. The latter thus offers an improvement in efficiency of 4·8 per cent. Related to the noise level of 94·8 per cent in the closed-plan office (100 per cent as a starting point) the improvement in efficiency (of 4·8 per cent) corresponds to a rise in output of 5 per cent. Related to 178 normal working hours in the month, this means a time saving of 534 min.

3.3.1.4 AIR-CONDITIONING
Strictly speaking the profitability reckoning for an air-conditioning plant should be made separately, because the closed-plan office is just as air-conditionable as the open-plan office and the success of an air-conditioning plant should not be attributed typically to the open-plan office. Many open-plan offices are capable of existing without an air-conditioning plant, although an optimally designed open-plan office requires one. If in this sense one is to consider the open-plan office as a complete and homogenous organizational element, it is acceptable to include the output advantages of air-conditioning in the profitability comparison, provided that the costs of the air-conditioning plant are accordingly included in the profitability account.

More than any other single factor the regional and local climate and temperature of a particular place and firm is responsible for the success of an air-conditioning plant. In one case of a large West German town in the Rhein-Ruhr region the following conditions were ascertained.

Temperature fluctuations in a conventional cellular-design high building were between 17 and 35°C (in summer), and the relative humidity fluctuations between 35 and 65 per cent. In contrast, an air-conditioning plant can offer the following values, to be considered as optimum for productivity:

Temperature in summer 21–24°C
Temperature in winter 20–22°C
Optimum temperature value 20·5°C
Average relative humidity 50 per cent

Fluctuations and deviations from the optimum value result in output losses. The influence of deviation from the optimum temperature value on efficiency can be deduced from the specific measurements shown in Table 3.14. On the basis of these temperature fluctuations, the fluctuation in efficiency is between 99·8 and 23 per cent, i.e. time losses attributable solely to temperature can vary between as much as 0·2 and 77 per cent (high temperatures above 30°C and correspondingly low

Table 3.14

| Temperature, °C | Efficiency, per cent | | |
| | Effective | Change | |
		Individual	Cumulative
16	96·3	1·4	3·7
17	97·7	1·0	2·3
18	98·7	0·7	1·3
19	99·4	0·4	0·6
20	99·8	0·2	0·2
20·5	100	0	0
21	99·7	0·3	0·3
22	99·2	0·5	0·8
23	98·4	0·8	1·6
24	97·2	1·2	2·8
25	95·5	1·7	4·5
30	82	13·5	18
35	61	21	39
40	23	38	77

Table 3.15

Temperature, °C	Days per year, approximate	Reduction in efficiency Individual, %	Reduction in efficiency Totalled
40	5	27	385
35	8	39	312
30	12	18	216
25	15	4·5	67
22–40	50	1·8	90
19–21	135	0·25	34
16–18	15	2·5	37
	240	4·8	1141

efficiency occur, of course, only for two months in the year and not always then). Temperature distribution is ascertained for the whole year and the corresponding fluctuation in efficiency is therefore as shown in Table 3.15. Accordingly, considered over the whole year, there is an average drop in output of 4·8 per cent as a result of deviation of the effective temperature from the optimum temperature.

The variation in humidity is less and does not have such an adverse effect on efficiency as the temperature fluctuations. Keeping the humidity at a constant optimum level by means of an air-conditioning plant produces an output increase of about 0·5 per cent.

The total outcome of air-conditioning is thus a rise in output of 5·3 per cent, which related to 178 normal working hours is 566 min per month per person.

3.3.1.5 VISUALLY STIMULATED SPREADING OF WORK LOAD
The open-plan office breeds loyalty and comradeship. It reveals the injustice of some departments being under pressure and having to work overtime, whilst neighbouring departments have little work and can go home punctually. Unequal work loads of this nature are embarrassing and encourage staff to offer their services to overworked departments as far as they are able. The work load is thus spread on a friendly mutual help basis. In this way work peaks are better overcome and under-employment is remedied. Output- and costs-wise this mutual assistance only shows itself in respect of under-employment. The quota of visible non-occupation—ascertained from records of time distribution as 5 per cent—is reduced by half in the open-plan office, i.e. 2·5 per cent = 267 min.

3.3.1.6 REDUCTION IN ABSENTEEISM FROM WORKING PLACES DURING WORKING HOURS

Records of time distribution show that absenteeism amounts to 15 per cent on an average. A third is necessary and two-thirds avoidable. In the open-plan office absence is more apparent than in the closed-plan office, and this encourages good attendance. However, this only applies when and whilst a competent departmental head is present in the office. Numerous observations confirm that the more frequently the superior is absent, the more often his staff are missing from their desks. For this reason it is not possible even in the open-plan office to eliminate avoidable absenteeism completely. The minimum value to be expected, however, is a reduction in absenteeism of 1 per cent; 107 min.

That one cannot achieve the reduction in absenteeism which is intrinsically possible, is due to a fact that cannot be blamed on the open-plan office. This is the modern tendency to replace individual work at one's own desk, for which one is solely responsible, by team work involving a great deal of discussion. The absence of the head or supervisor from the department unfortunately has a demoralizing effect on the personnel.

3.3.1.7 REDUCTION IN PRIVATE OCCUPATIONS
The following time spent was recorded:

Private telephoning	2 per cent
Private conversation	7 per cent
Private business	3 per cent
	—
Private occupations	12 per cent

The open-plan office trains people to restrict private occupations. The saving is at least 2 per cent = 213 min.

3.3.1.8 DRAWING ON OUTPUT RESERVES
In concerns with an average, i.e. moderate, working climate and in office undertakings conducted normally, i.e. without exact and daily checked output targets, the office employee works to only about 75 per cent of his capacity. This has been proved by countless comparisons of output studies and average outputs. Though reserve of output amounts to 25 per cent on average, it should be individually determined for each concern. Without time studies one can ascertain the output reserve as a mean value between visible time losses and the maximum time loss

determinable from the output variance. In the present case the output reserve was 16 per cent. In the open-plan office, part of the output reserve is drawn on voluntarily by the staff for the same reason that stimulates spread of work load: loyalty in the open-plan office causes people not only to take on others' work but also to make an increased output effort in order to master an exceptional load and show particularly noticeable outputs in jobs when other people can see them being done. By far the greater part of the output reserve can be exploited by organizational measures to control output. Utilization of output reserves solely through the training influence of the open-plan office amounts to 2 per cent = 213 min/month.

The sum total of these forms of increased output gives a time saving of 2,122 min/month per person in a normal working period of 178 hr.

3.3.2 Reduced output

The open-plan office has only two essential disadvantages: greater secondary distraction causing output and time losses, and a decline in status symbols, although this latter point does not have any perceptible influence on workers' output. The theoretical danger, expressed frequently by sceptics, of greater absenteeism, during and after acquisition of an open-plan office, has in practice not proved to be true. Less individual status has thus not resulted in absenteeism nor in a daily awareness of less individual importance and has therefore not caused a diminution in work motivation. (The general prestige of the undertaking or the department housed in an open-plan office is considerably enhanced, but this does not affect the individual performance of the staff.)

3.3.2.1 GREATER SECONDARY DISTRACTION

In closed-plan offices, persons walking past are screened off by corridor walls. In open-plan offices they cause frequent and sometimes extensive visual stimuli, disturbances and distraction. Through observations five disturbing actions perceptible to everyone in the open-plan office have been recorded hourly. Nine hundred disturbances monthly @ 8 sec time loss constitutes a reduction in output of 120 min/month per person. Experience has shown that office employees carrying out mentally creative work are much more susceptible to disturbances than persons performing routine mechanical tasks. Likewise male employees more than females.

Apart from this no reductions in output attributable to the environmental influences of the open-plan office have been ascertained.

3.3.3 Conclusion

Setting off increases and reductions in output against one another in an output balance sheet gives a result positively in favour of the open-plan office (see Table 3.16). This comparison of output gives an output gain to the open-plan office of 18·7 per cent. Related to the average costs for one office employee of DM 12,000 per year, this equals DM 2,244 productivity per person per year. In an administrative concern comprising only 100 persons this could still compensate for DM 224,400 higher building costs of an open-plan office.

Although the surveys and measurements carried out in this individual study leave little to be desired in the way of thoroughness, time calculations and costs, they do not justify generalization. The composition of the various heads proves that output values may differ greatly in every case. Time distribution studies supply varying crucial points and overall results in different concerns. Voluntary drawing on output reserves and voluntary work load spread are strongly dependent on the work situation, the staff structure, the style of direction and the working and management atmosphere. Reduction of absenteeism and private occupations is a function of work organization and intensity of direction. Noise disturbance depends on the mechanical equipment of the individual concern and frequency of telephonic communication. The success of air-conditioning is dependent on local temperature fluctuations and climatic conditions. Disturbance factors influencing secondary distraction and causing reduction in output are determined on the one hand by the functions, attention to work and qualifications of the personnel, and on the other by the type, sex and frequency of the disturbing or distracting elements.

Starting from the usual conditions of a normal office concern one can assume that under no circumstances will the reductions in output caused by the open-plan office be greater as a whole than the increases in output. All the same, these individual influencing factors may effect such a considerable variation in output gain that the net productivity of an open-plan office may embrace a range of 5 to 25 per cent. According to the author's personal observations (which, however, were less thorough than the foregoing study), the effective gain in optimally designed open-plan offices is 16 per cent on average.

Table 3.16 Output balance sheet for the open-plan office per employee

	Credit: increased output			Debit: decreased output	
No.	*Heading and calculation*	*Gain min/month*	*No.*	*Heading*	*Loss, min/month*
1	Better communication; elimination of 640 door movements and short journeys per employee; reduction of wrong calls	80	1	Greater secondary distraction 900 disturbances at 8 sec	120
2	Less primary distraction through telephone calls and visitors	142			
3	Less noise disturbances; rise in output from 94·8 to 99·6 per cent	534			
4	Optimum air-conditioning; rise in output due to:				
	optimum temperature regulation 4·8 per cent	513			
	optimum air moisture 0·5 per cent	53			
5	Visually stimulated spread of work load 2·5 per cent	267			
6	Reduction in absenteeism, at least 1 per cent	107			
7	Reduction in private occupations at least 2 per cent	213			
8	Drawing on output reserves 2 per cent	213		Output gain (18·7 per cent)	2,002
	Total	2,122		Total	2,122

A regrettable fact, however, is that many undertakings after installing open-plan offices in their administrative building, do not ascertain and therefore do not exploit this output gain. The entire office staff unconsciously produce an increased output which is not noticed. If no demands are made on a proffered output, it dries up within a short time, the output settles down at the lower level of less pressure. In the course of time it becomes static at this level. A later sudden or gradual increase in the amount of work is then viewed from the now established routine level. It is felt to be an additional load which is no longer met from the intrinsic reserve but achieved by additional staff or by mechanization incurring capital expenditure. Such a development can in no way be blamed on the open-plan office, however.

In spite of all reservations in the face of the array of figures submitted on costs and output, the general conclusion in the majority of cases must be that the open-plan office is profitable. If the criteria of building and maintenance costs and staff output may be taken as a measure of the profitability of open-plan premises*, the result of the foregoing investigations is the monetarily assessable profitability formula:

$$\frac{\text{Reduced costs of open-plan premises}}{\text{Increased productivity of open-plan premises}}$$
$$= \text{Profitability of open-plan premises}$$

Even in the case of occasional increased cost of the open-plan office, the increased productivity may compensate for this and maintain the over-all result. The numerical values to be inserted as the numerator and denominator of the above fraction must be left to the individual concern in question.

* According to Funke [7, p 113], the criterion for the profitability of an office building is 'how far it contributes to the success of the concern'. However, he leaves open how the success of the concern and the share of the office building in this success is to be measured.

Chapter 4

Psychological problems

Although it is now 11 years since the open-plan movement began, the open-plan office is still a phenomenon beset with problems. It would be quite wrong to try in 1969 to claim wholehearted acceptance of the open-plan office by large numbers of office workers. In an internal opinion poll conducted among more than 1,500 employees of a large administrative concern in Münster, 97·5 per cent spontaneously declared their categorical rejection of the proposed open-plan office. Rosner [35] reports other surveys, according to which as recently as 1967, 99 per cent female and 97 per cent male employees were still not prepared to work voluntarily in an open-plan office. Rosner is right to raise against such statements of opinion the objection that 'of those who reject the open-plan office, scarcely a single person has ever worked in one'. There is no need to seek external causes for the general rejection of the open-plan office. Even the Deutsche Angestellten-Gewerkschaft and the Deutsche Gewerkschafts-Bund (German Employees' Union and Federation of German Trade Unions), whilst objectively weighing up the pros and cons, are generally in favour of the open-plan office [36–38]. It has not been possible to ascertain the outside influences on office employees from any source.

Even among open-plan office users, who may in some cases have been working in them for 8 to 10 years, one does not detect burning enthusiasm for the open-plan office. This is found only among managers, office planners and architects, who plan and design such offices. The large majority of open-plan users tolerate the open-plan office without delighting in it. They recognize its advantages and become used to its disadvantages. Teething troubles and initial difficulties are overcome and the open-plan office is accepted as an economic necessity. Even in open-plan offices which are optimally designed from organizational and technical standpoints, approval of the open-plan office is moderate, not rapturous—as shown by the DIB (Deutsche Institut für Betriebswirtschaft—German Institute for Industrial Economy) text published in this book. A latent sympathy for the closed-plan office and a continual striving for the single room still glimmer in the minds of office employees.

There is no hope of eradicating this mental tendency within a reasonable time; it is too deep-rooted. Only after decades and generations can one expect a structural change in mentality.

The forceful psychological objections raised after acquisition of an open-plan office can be powerful and disturbing. Every manager and office planner should be prepared for them. There are as many objections to the acquisition of an open-plan office as there are motives for human dissatisfaction. An inexhaustible supply of unkind words is drawn upon, for example 'impersonal mass work-room', 'American atmosphere', 'it's like sitting in a glass box', 'one is constantly supervised', 'canned air', 'witnessing of terrible arguments between superiors and subordinates or between colleagues is distressing', 'it's like a cycle stadium', 'you have the feeling of being in a bunker or the underground', 'I feel as if I have been transferred for disciplinary reasons', 'the change from a single to an open-plan office constitutes a loss of prestige and authority', 'I would not tell my student friends that I work in an open-plan office', 'one is just a number', 'respect for women is lost; that is not made up for by the walnut desk, I am treated just like anyone else', and many more. All these varied statements have a basis of emotional anxiety—the anxiety of mass isolation. The industrial psychologist has this to say [39]:

> 'Deep psychological probing with judicious questioning clearly reveals that the motives of rejection are exclusively emotional and are bound up with characteristic, historically induced misconceptions. . . . Again and again it has been found that the keynote of well-being in one's place of work is a sense of living room comfort. This feeling of well-being is promoted by the closely coupled features of a relatively small area and the closeness of one or more colleagues. . . . People would rather put up with the atmosphere of a submarine, or a polar expedition (in the closed-plan office), would rather be disturbed by a neighbour on the telephone (in the closed-plan office), tolerate the intermittent high noise level and continual bustle in a confined space (in the closed-plan office), than have to be alone. The danger of large numbers is not massing, but loss of independence, isolation and reduction of human contact (in the open-plan office).'

Although it is true in the open-plan office that group consciousness is strengthened through grouping of workplaces and by screens, and that communication with other departments is improved, it is precisely there that the employee feels in a strange way the loss of independence in the mass. Of all emotional fears this is the one to prove utterly unfounded after some time spent working in an open-plan office.

A number of other psychological motives create further prejudices of staff against the open-plan office: the need for self-importance motivates the necessity for the independent, individual character of the single room; the idea of homeliness longs to be enclosed by four walls; the need for security requires a solid wall at one's back; the individualistic tendency inherent in the German office worker strives for an individual atmosphere and isolation, particularly in the case of sensitive executive staff; the need for clique-forming finds a firm basis in the closed-plan office; only in the closed-plan office are private occupations, idleness and lack of supervision undiscovered or tolerated by a few colleagues guilty of the same offences; natural human inertia is generally speaking a hindrance to the introduction of the open-plan office. The final goal of every office employee is the single room, because it counts as a prestige feature and as a status symbol, it is also a bolster for authority and 'often a carefully preserved badge of rank' [40].

There is little point in trying to refute these objections particularly as, as a rule, they remain unspoken and are merely the invisible force behind tenuous superficial arguments. Such emotionally and psychologically based prejudices are not amenable to reasonable discussion in the concern. Rosner states quite rightly [41] that 'every question of environment . . . is answered first with the emotions and then with reason. This also applies to each individual's decision for or against the open-plan office,' and he asks that the subject be treated objectively. Nor is one usually successful in combating mistrust and scepticism with words, when trying to prove that groupings and 'subjective areas' can be created as intimate zones just as well in the open-plan office as in the closed-plan office [3, pp 515 and 518]:

'Work in groups provides social stimulus. Here the working units are made visible, either by common alignment of the furniture or by demarcating cupboards and plant troughs. Such group signs promote a feeling of solidarity. . . . Such subjective areas of the office landscape create, together with the sense of belonging to a working group, a feeling of intimacy. . . . Their (the employees') desire for intimacy is a valid one, because it generates spiritual forces. . . . The basic units of the office landscape within one's perception and experience are the subjective areas. . . . We must not expect every section of an open-plan office to be fully visible.'

Most psychological resistance shows itself as resentment, which disappears automatically soon after occupation of the open-plan office. Nevertheless, employees occupying an open-plan office should not be constantly and painfully reminded of the class difference between the open-plan office and the closed office or single room. If various single rooms or closed-plan offices remain as status symbols for privileged workers on the same floor as an open-plan office, they constitute a continual provocation of the workers in the open-plan office, constantly fanning the flame of dissatisfaction and disrupting the working atmosphere, until sooner or later the open-plan office is replaced by closed-plan offices or the closed-plan offices are pulled down. Above all, senior staff must set a good example. That directors and executives can work in the open-plan offices is proved by numerous examples: such as Orenstein-Koppel und Lübecker Maschinebau AG (Dortmund), Nino (Nordhorn), Verlag Buch und Ton (Gütersloh) and others [42].

The initial difficulties of an open-plan office must be met with patience. Many voices may be raised in protest, threatening resignation, strikes and sabotage; emotional tension runs high; general and departmental meetings are stirred up by radical agitators; actual physiological disturbances occur even. The staff complain of headaches (because they are not used to the air-conditioning), men and women suffer from agoraphobia (because of the unaccustomed size of the area) and are constantly stating 'there's a draught', although it can be proved by a lighted match that there is not a breath of air moving in the room; the new sound level is perceived as unbearable noise; the screens are called 'Berlin Walls'; the staff feel—with some justification—that they are being observed, as if they are on display. Movements, and visitors to the office, lead to considerable difficulties in concentration. All these facts may contribute to a considerable temporary drop in output (of up to 50 per cent). All stories should be listened to patiently but without attributing dramatic significance to them. After three to six months these phenomena will have disappeared and output will settle down to a normal level or above.

Objective technical faults are a different matter. Where draughts and smells can be objectively found in the open-plan office, or where temperatures are too high or too low, the air-conditioning must be technically improved. Where lighting is glaring, too strong or too weak, the light fittings must be changed. Where noise is found by objective measurements to be too loud, too intermittent, too shrill or too soft, the sound-proofing must be improved by screens and curtains and other measures and noisy telephone users and speakers must be trained to speak softly. Where the workplace arrangement does not do justice to the work flow or is subject to too great a disturbance, it must be altered.

Should the open-plan office subsequently prove to be objectively unsuitable for certain special workplaces, appropriate total screening must be effected, or in exceptional cases certain functions must be removed from the open-plan office and accommodated in single rooms or closed-plan offices. Such an exception can be conceded for highly concentrated creative work that cannot tolerate the slightest distraction. In such a case visual disturbances and other distractions could cause an uneconomic impairment of output. Business negotiations and important or confidential discussions can, as testified by unanimous experience in several undertakings, take place without difficulty in an open-plan office behind screens. Nevertheless a closed office that can be locked is probably best in cases of maximum secrecy and confidence.

It is, however, ridiculous to expect nothing but unmitigated advantage from the open-plan office. Some negative sides can be discovered to every positive situation. An air-conditioning plant, for example, whilst extracting stale air and cigarette smoke, also removes the fragrance of flowers and perfume: 'The air-conditioned room smells of nothing' [40].

Office planners must hold on firmly to clearly recognized advantages and necessary features. If, for example, objections are raised to screens ('like wearing blinkers') one must remain convinced that movable partitions are necessary for sound-proofing and visual screening and because of psychological considerations (need for security, need for prestige, etc.). Although the DAG (German Employees' Union) chief once said of the firm of Helmut Horten (Düsseldorf): 'All the offices in that firm are carpeted and equipped with wardrobes, they have teak-panelled walls and flower arrangements, and a rest hall as comfortable as a hotel lounge—so what?', one must consider these features as an indispensable part of the modern office landscape, as necessary sound-proofing measures and psychological substitutes. (The reply of Horten's General Secretary, Eckelmann, to that was: 'When we take something away from you, we must give you something in exchange.' If in a particular concern tending of one's own flowers, or a pronounced prestige consciousness is a positive component of the general working atmosphere, one should try to take these requirements into account in the open-plan office. It is still possible for flowers brought to work to be arranged and tended in freely distributed plant troughs, still possible to allow a senior employee an Oriental carpet and a particularly comfortable chair. Status is a necessary part of human relationship, an important means of showing rank in a hierarchy and the outer trappings of authority. No period of human history has been without assumption of status and it would be fatal to ignore this state of affairs in the open-plan office. Helmut Sopp once said, 'Influence is worth more than money.'

All this apart, human beings are not so inflexible that they cannot adapt. The new working atmosphere and the new form of community generate such diverse impulses in the persons working in them that in the end they cannot escape their influence. A new type of office user evolves from the open-plan office: he speaks more softly; he is more considerate; he dresses correctly and carefully; arguments are conducted at a calmer pitch; unpleasant scenes finally disappear.

Psychological resistance can be considerably weakened if a deliberate staff propaganda campaign is incorporated in the office planning, in four stages.

1 PSYCHOLOGICAL PREPARATION At an early stage the personnel should be prepared for the new office atmosphere. A lecture to the employees with slides will give them some idea of what an open-plan office is like. Visits to one or two new open-plan office buildings by the staff or selected workers provide the first personal impression which, if the concerns are well-chosen, will always be a positive one. Interviews or questionnaires asking for the faults of the present spatial arrangement open eyes to critical aspects and create readiness for change.

Under no circumstances should employees be subjected to an opinion poll asking what they think of open-plan offices.

2 PLANNING Selected employees' representatives may be included in the planning. They can be of assistance in discussion of communication problems, and give valuable advice on the planning of department and workplace layout; they may be consulted on evaluation of new furniture and on the colour of carpeting, ceilings, walls and other paintwork.

3 MOVING Every single employee should participate in the move. He should pack the contents of his own workplace in the removal

cartons and take them out again in the new office to arrange them in the new furniture (if new furniture has been acquired).

4 FOLLOW-UP Four weeks after the move internal discussions about faults discovered can take place at a departmental level. This gives the employees an opportunity of letting off steam officially and at the same time putting forward objective faults rationally. The process can be repeated after three months. Personal discussion can be supplemented by a test sheet procedure (see Fig. 2), in which mostly concrete and material defects are brought to light.

Even if all these measures aimed at personal involvement during the planning period and during and after the move make no real productive contribution, they have a very reassuring effect on the personnel. Since it has been proved by psychologists and doctors that illnesses and physiological disturbances can in many cases be caused solely by mental tension, the removal or attenuation of such tensions may help to avoid damage to health*.

* Helmut Sopp: 'The introduction of optimum lighting by fluorescent tubes can, if it has not been prepared for by suitable propaganda, be met by headaches, distortions of vision and general discomfort' [39].

TEST SHEET	Re: Open-plan office	To	From	Department	Date
			(*may be omitted*)		
1 What I do not like:			How I would improve it:		Person assuming responsibility for carrying into effect:
2 What I like:			Other remarks:		
Already discussed with:			Signature:		Seen and acted upon:
			(*may be omitted*)		*Head of Department*

Fig. 2 Follow-up test sheet

Chapter 5

Summary

The open-plan office constitutes an important advance in business organization. When of adequate size and optimum technical and organizational design, the open-plan office helps lower costs and increase output. Numerous disadvantages of the closed-plan office are avoided in the open-plan office. Against this the open-plan office has few disadvantages*.

The many disadvantages that can be levelled against the closed-plan office are as follows:

1 Long and involved journeys of staff through many rooms and floors.
2 Verbal information and discussions are made difficult by distances and lack of visibility. This leads to long journeys, wasted telephone calls and avoidable memoranda.
3 A free, assymetrical layout of workplaces and operation of appliances is often impossible. The journey to machines, filing cabinets and other appliances causes frequent standing, time losses and fatigue.
4 Interchange of working appliances, e.g. dictating machines, copying machines, etc., is hindered and made difficult.
5 The arrangement of desks in the closed-plan office necessitates standard measurements, which are not always functionally desirable for the members of the working group or the individual workplace.
6 There is a high degree of primary distraction in the office from the telephone and visitors†.
7 There is greater noise because of the higher proportion of wall per square metre with resultant higher sound frequency.

* At a conference of DAG (German Employees' Union) in Ludwigshafen at the Badische Anilin- und Sodafabrike, Prof. Curt Siegel (TH Stuttgart) warned people against seeing the open-plan office either as exclusively good or as exclusively bad—in other words, either as a blessing or a curse. The open-plan office is predominantly good.

† Wolfgang Schnelle writes: 'Willingness to work is constantly dampened if not completely destroyed by disturbances of noise, light, vision and air' [43, p 17].

8 There are extreme light contrasts through the constant change from room light (300–500 lx) to daylight (3,000–10,000 lx) and vice versa. The visual nerves tire more quickly than at a constant level of say either 500 or 10,000 lx.

9 There are continual draughts from opened doors or windows.

10 Wasted dead angles behind doors and at the four corners of the closed office cause space losses and encourage the accumulation of rubbish.

11 Formation of groups beyond one set of four walls, and loyalty to neighbouring departments are made difficult.

12 No automatic spread of work load takes place between neighbouring departments.

13 There are high time losses through private occupations, lack of work load spread, frequent absence and all the other aforementioned reasons.

14 In the closed-plan office considerable difficulties may arise within the working group because of people who are different or incompatible. This increases the need to be absent.

15 The closed-plan office cements differences of rank and class*.

16 Adaptation to changing department sizes, work functions, auxiliary aids and working methods is made difficult because of the inflexibility of solid or even sectional walls.

17 Administrative buildings of cellular design with closed-plan offices to the left and right of a central corridor always have three parallel corridors (the central one and the corridors running parallel into the rooms on the left and right), with resultant high space losses.

Against these numerous disadvantages there are a few advantages of the closed-plan office:

1 The closed-plan office offers higher individual prestige than the individual workplace in the open-plan office.

2 A 100 per cent total screening in respect of visibility, noise and other disturbances is possible only in the closed-plan office.

* 'The preference for distinguishing badges of rank to the detriment of communicative co-operation is one of the mainsprings of bureaucracy; this manifests itself in a multiplication of memoranda (instead of verbal exchange), the lengthening of "official channels" (instead of direct information) and also in a formalizing of interpersonal relations' [43, p 22]. This statement is correct but one should add that the effects mentioned are to be attributed not only to the closed-plan design but also generally to the growing size of firms and administrations.

3 Differentiated ranking can be shown in a greater number of ways in the closed-plan office than in the open plan*.

Many disadvantages of the closed-plan office can be turned to advantages in the open-plan office:

1 Space-saving.
2 Saving in building costs.
3 Lower fitting out costs (larger and continuous light fittings, no walls and doors, cheaper laying of flooring).
4 Lower maintenance costs.
5 Elimination of conversion costs.
6 Greater flexibility of departments and workplaces.
7 Less noise.
8 Improved lighting through large-scale distribution of light fittings.
9 Better overlooking facilities, hence reduction of wrong calls and simpler supervision, improved information exchange.
10 Better communication for staff contacts and personal discussion, promotion of team spirit.
11 Better conditions for continuous work flow and for connecting departments by mechanical conveyors.
12 Less time lost through less absence from desks, fewer private occupations and less idleness.
13 Greater community spirit, improved loyalty.
14 Less primary distraction than in the multi-person closed-plan office.
15 Large-scale prestige spatial layout with increased prestige to the undertaking and the departments as a whole.
16 Greater discipline in behaviour and clothing.

Even if one disregards the temporary difficulties of preparation for and introduction of the open-plan office and considers the situation only after an introductory period of six to eight months from moving into the open-plan office, the following disadvantages must still be mentioned:

1 Greater secondary distraction from staff and visitors outside the department.
2 Less concentration for mentally creative workers.
3 Less status of the individual workplace.
4 Difficulties with people who speak loudly.
5 An air-conditioning plant does not allow temperature regulation to

* See, on the cubicle system [20, p 12] and on cellular construction [1, p 21].

individual tastes as in the single room. The same temperature has a different effect on persons of different sex and different ages.

6 Greater changeover and adaptation difficulties.

It is not necessary just to quote the small number of disadvantages in order to prove the superiority of the open-plan office by the much larger number of advantages. Unsubstantiated verbal arguments are not hard currency. The advantages which can be demonstrated numerically prove the open-plan office's superiority by lower over-all costs and higher productivity. Only with monetarily ascertained unprofitability would one use the superior number of verbal arguments to sway opinion in favour of the open-plan office. Greater profitability of the closed-plan office or greater weight of verbal arguments in its favour remain restricted to individual, exceptional cases.

For the majority of all administrative concerns and departments the open-plan office remains the most profitable solution.

Optimum ground plan
formulated for an office building planned by the
Axel Boje Unternehmungs-Beratung, Düsseldorf, in 1967

by H. Merkel (Architect) and H. Merten (Mathematician)

Problem

To find the optimum number of floors needed in an office building of given total area to minimize the time taken to travel from any one point to all other points. Total area $=40{,}000$ m^2.

Symbols

Total area	$F=40{,}000$ m^2
Number of floors	n
Distance between floors	$h_G=3{\cdot}60$ m
Floor radius	R
Number of lifts	f
Lift speed	$V_{max}=4$ m/sec
Walking speed	$V_w=1$ m/sec

Simplification

The form of the floor area is a circle with radius R:

$$n\pi R^2 = F$$
$$R = (F/n\pi)^{\frac{1}{2}}$$

Calculation of the average travelling time from all points of the circle to the centre (Fig 2):

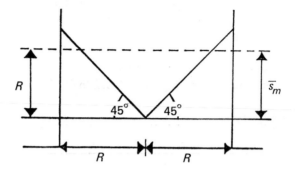

Fig. 2

$\bar{s}_m$ is the average distance of all points from the centre:

$$Z_R - K_R = Z\bar{s}_m$$
$$\pi R^3 - \tfrac{1}{3}\pi R^3 = \pi R^2 \bar{s}_m$$
$$\bar{s}_m = \tfrac{2}{3}R$$
$$V_w = 1 \text{ m/sec}$$
$$\bar{t}_m = \bar{s}_m / V_w = \tfrac{2}{3}R = \tfrac{2}{3}(F/n\pi)^{\frac{1}{2}} \text{ sec}$$

Calculation of the average travelling time from all points of the circle to one another (Fig. 3):

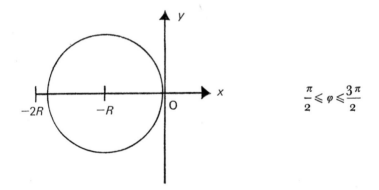

Fig. 3

$$(x+R)^2 + y^2 = R^2$$
$$(\varphi \cos \varphi + R)^2 + \rho^2 \sin^2 \varphi = R^2$$
$$\rho^2 + 2\rho r \cos \varphi = 0$$
$$\rho = -2R \cos \varphi$$

$$2\int_{\pi/2}^{\pi}\int_{0}^{-2R\cos\varphi}\rho^2\,\mathrm{d}\rho\,\mathrm{d}\varphi=\frac{2}{3}\int_{\pi/2}^{\pi}\Big[-2\,R\cos\varphi\Big]^3\mathrm{d}\varphi=\frac{16}{3}\,R^3\int_{\pi/2}^{\pi}\cos^3\varphi\,\mathrm{d}\varphi$$

$$=\times\frac{16}{3}\,R^3(\sin\varphi-\tfrac{1}{3}\sin^3\varphi)\;\Big|_{\pi/2}^{\pi}$$

$$=\times\frac{16}{3}\,R^3\left(-\frac{2}{3}\right)$$

$$=32R^3/9$$

$$\pi R^2\bar{s}_R=\frac{32}{9}R^3$$

$$\bar{s}_R=\frac{32}{9\pi}R$$

$\bar{s}_R$ is the average distance of all points from the peripheral point (Fig. 4):

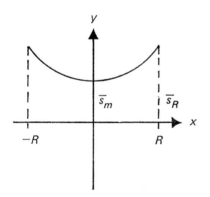

$$y=ax^2+b$$
$$x=0\quad b=\bar{s}_m=\tfrac{2}{3}\,R$$

$$x=R\bar{s}_R\;=aR^2+\tfrac{2}{3}R$$

$$a=\frac{1}{R}\left(\frac{32}{9\pi}-\frac{2}{3}\right)$$

$$\bar{s}_R=\frac{32}{9\pi}\,R$$

Fig. 4

$$y=\frac{1}{R}\left(\frac{32}{9\pi}-\frac{2}{3}\right)x^2+\frac{2}{3}\,R$$

$$V_P=\pi\int_{0}^{R}x^2f'\,(x)\,\mathrm{d}x$$

73

$$= 2\pi \frac{1}{R}\left(\frac{32}{9\pi} - \frac{2}{3}\right)\int_0^R x^3\,dx$$

$$= \frac{1}{2}\ \pi R^3\ \left(\frac{32}{9\pi} - \frac{2}{3}\right)$$

$$\bar{z}\bar{s}_R - V_P = \bar{z}\bar{s}_E$$

$$\pi R^2 \bar{s}_E = \frac{32}{9\pi}\ R^3\pi - \tfrac{1}{2}\pi R^3\left(\frac{32}{9\pi}\ \frac{2}{3}\right)$$

$$\bar{s}_E = \frac{32}{9\pi} - \left(\frac{32}{9\pi} - \frac{2}{3}\right)\tfrac{1}{2}R$$

$$\bar{s}_E = \left(\frac{16}{9\pi} + \frac{1}{3}\right)R$$

$$\bar{t}_E = \bar{s}_E/V_W = \left(\frac{16}{9\pi} + \frac{1}{3}\right)\ (F/n\pi)^{\frac{1}{2}}$$

$$= 0{\cdot}9(F/n\pi)^{\frac{1}{2}}\ \text{sec}$$

Calculation of the average travelling time in lift; h_F is the average height travelled:

$$\bar{h}_F = \frac{\displaystyle\sum_{i=1}^{1}i + \sum_{i=1}^{2}i + \sum_{i=1}^{3}i + \dots \sum_{i=1}^{n-1}i}{\displaystyle\sum_{i=1}^{n-1}i}h_G$$

$$= \frac{n+1}{3}\ h_G$$

$$\bar{t}_F = \frac{\bar{h}_F}{v} = \frac{n+1}{12}\ h_G\ \text{sec}$$

Determination of the average call time; h_R = average call height. The following formula applies:

$$\bar{h}_R = \frac{1}{n^{f+1}}\sum_{i=1}^{m}[n(n-2i+1)^f + 2i(n-2i)^f]h_G$$

$$m = n/2 \text{ for even } n$$
$$m = (n-1)/2 \text{ for odd } n$$

With the aid of a diagram the following values were plotted.

$n \backslash f$	1	2	3	4	5
1	0	0	0	0	0
2	0·5	0·25	0·125	0·063	0·031
3	0·889	0·519	0·321	0·206	0·134
4	1·25	0·75	0·5	0·352	0·254
5	1·6	0·976	0·67	0·488	0·37
6	1·944	1·194	0·83	0·62	0·48
7	2·29	1·41	0·99	0·747	0·588
8	2·63	1·625			
9	2·96				
10	3·3				

These values were extrapolated as a graph (see Fig. 5). From the graph

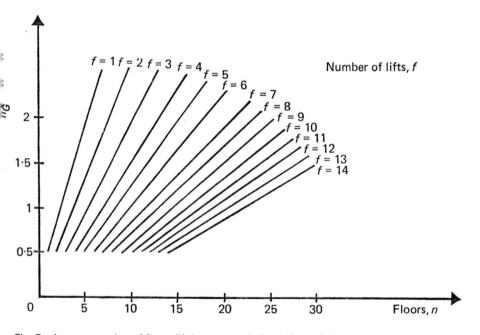

Fig. 5   Average number of floors lift has to travel after being called

75

one obtains the following equations. For $f = 10$

$$\bar{h}_R = (0\cdot0543n - 0\cdot13)h_G$$
$$E_R = \bar{h}_R/V$$
$$= \tfrac{1}{4}(0\cdot0543n - 0\cdot13)h_G \text{ sec}$$
$$\bar{s}_R = an + b$$
$$b = -0\cdot13$$
$$a = 1/(30 - 11\cdot6) = 0\cdot0543$$

Ascertaining of optimum times

$$\bar{t}_{total} = \frac{\bar{t}_E + (n-1)(2\bar{t}_m + \bar{t}_R + \bar{t}_F + t_V)}{n}$$

t_v = time losses

entering time	$t_e = 1\cdot1$ sec
leaving time	$t_l = 1\cdot0$ sec
opening time	$t_o = 1\cdot75$ sec
closing time	$t_c = 1\cdot75$ sec
slowing down time	$t_s = 3\cdot1$ sec
accelerating time	$t_a = 3\cdot1$ sec

$$t_v = t_e + t_l + 2t_o + t_c + 2t_s + 2t_a$$
$$= 19\cdot75 \text{ sec}$$

$$\bar{t}_{total}(n) = \frac{1}{n}\left\{ 0\cdot9 \left(\frac{F}{n\pi}\right)^{\frac{1}{2}} \right.$$

$$+ (n-1)\left[\frac{4}{3}\left(\frac{F}{n\pi}\right)^{\frac{1}{2}} + \tfrac{1}{4}h_G(0\cdot0543n - 0\cdot13) \right.$$

$$\left. \left. + \frac{n+1}{12}h_G + 19\cdot75 \right] \right\}$$

$$= (0\cdot9 - 3/4)\left(\frac{F}{\pi}\right)^{\frac{1}{2}}\frac{1}{n^{3/2}} + \frac{4}{3}\left(\frac{F}{\pi}\right)^{\frac{1}{2}}\frac{1}{n^{\frac{1}{2}}}$$

$$+ \left(\frac{0\cdot0543}{4} + \frac{1}{12}\right)h_G n + \left[\left(\frac{0\cdot13}{4} - \frac{1}{12}\right)h_G - 19\cdot75\right]\frac{1}{n}$$

$$+ \left(19\cdot75 - \frac{0\cdot0543 + 0\cdot13}{4}h_G\right)$$

$$= -48 \cdot 9 \frac{1}{n^{3/2}} - 19 \cdot 93 \frac{1}{n} + 150 \cdot 45 \frac{1}{n^{\frac{1}{2}}} + 0 \cdot 349n + 19 \cdot 584$$

$$\frac{d\bar{t}_{total}}{dn} = 73 \cdot 34 \frac{1}{n^{5/2}} + 19 \cdot 93 \frac{1}{n^2} + 75 \cdot 23 \frac{1}{n^{3/2}} + 0 \cdot 349$$

$$\frac{d\bar{t}_{total}}{dn} = 0$$

Multiplication by $n^{5/2}$ and substitution of $n^{\frac{1}{2}} = x$ gives

$$0 \cdot 349x^5 - 75 \cdot 23x^2 + 19 \cdot 93x + 73 \cdot 34 = 0$$
$$x = 5 \cdot 845$$
$$n = 34 \cdot 16$$

The optimum number of floors, as specified in the problem, is thus $n = 34$. This result assumes ideal lift operation (no intermediate stops, low access quota, optimum allotment of calls, minimum time losses). Every disturbance factor in operation (not only of a technical nature) shifts the optimum in the direction of a smaller number of floors. For a graph of the time function see Fig. 6.

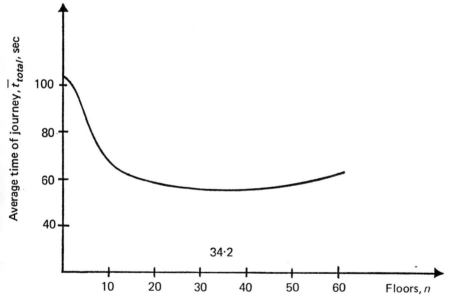

Fig. 6   Average time of journeys

The optimum floor area of each floor F_G with one central set of services, i.e. one technical core, is obtained from:

$$F_G = 40,000/24 = 1,176 \text{ m}^2$$

Area measurements and building costs for office workplaces and office premises

Compiled by Axel Boje, Düsseldorf

Size

M. Fischer	250–3,000 m²
Reznik	From 324 (18 × 18) m²
DAG Deutsche Angestellten-Gewerkschaft	From 400 (20 × 20) m²
Henn (1955)	From 200 m²
Henn (1964)	From 600 m²
Boje	From 200 m²
Tiedemann (16 workplaces)	From 160 m²
Gottschalk	600–1,000 m²
Schmalenbach-Gesellschaft	400–1,300 m²

Spatial measurements

Window axis interval	1·50–1·60–3·20	AWV*
	1·30 or 2·60	Rosenkranz
	1·95	KGVV†
	1·25–1·875–2·50	Neufert
	2·00 favoured	Rimpl
	1·60–2·00 elsewhere	Rimpl
	2·20 beside furniture in rear	Rimpl
	1·30–1·50	
	1·58–1·88–1·97	Joedicke
	1·48–1·83	Ripen (USA)

* AWV = Ausschuss für wirtschaftliche Verwaltung (Frankfurt).
† KGVV = Kommunale Gemeinschaftsstelle für Verwaltungs-Vereinfachung (Köln).

	1·53–1·57	Divers architects
	1·66	Divers architects
	1·63	Badische Analin- und Sodafabrik (Ludwigshafen)
	1·70–2·25	Schmalenbach-Gesellschaft
Static axial dimension	6·00 favoured	Rimpl
Supporting pillar interval	1·75–1·80–2·50–3·50–3·70–4·40	AWV
	1·30	Rosenkranz
Room length	2·60	Rosenkranz
	3·90	KGVV
Room depth (width)	4·10–5·00–5·60	AWV
	2·30	Rosenkranz
	5·30–5·50	KGVV
	6·00	Rimpl
	4·00–5·00–6·00	Joedicke
Main aisle width	2·00–2·50	Schmalenbach-Gesellschaft
Basic screen measurements	1·95 × 1·95 m	Voko-Modul
	0·39 m	
	0·78 m	
	1·56 m etc.	
	1·829 m	Connecticut Life Insurance Modul
	0·625 m	Neufert
	1·25 m	Neufert
	2·5 m	Neufert
	5·0 m	Neufert
	2·0 m	Rimpl
	2·60 × 2·30 m	Rosenkranz
Storey height: without air-conditioning in the ceiling	3·4 × 4·2 m	
with air-conditioning in the ceiling	4·0 × 4·7 m	
Room height (inside measurement)	3·0 × 3·5 m	KGVV
	2·7 × 3·0 m	Gottschalk

	2·90 min.	Rimpl
	3·20–3·50 m	(Kleinraum-Büro) Schmalenbach-Gesellschaft
Distance of furniture from outside wall	0·50 m	Rimpl
	0·20 m	Joedicke
	0·50 m	Joedicke—near furniture or outside wall (without furniture)
	0·60 m	Joedicke—except corridors
Distance of furniture from other furniture, e.g. a cupboard	1·50 m	Rimpl
Side aisle and furniture access area	1·82–1·88 m	Joedicke
Depth for sitting and moving area	0·80 m	Rimpl—without filing cabinet or similar
	1·00 m	Rimpl—near filing cabinet or similar
	0·70–0·85 m	Joedicke—with or without filing cabinet or similar, without filing cabinet
	0·65 m	Schnelle—near movable revolving chair
	0·70 m	Schnelle—near revolving chair
	0·80 m	Schnelle—near simple chair

Workplace area

1. *Net area per workplace*

Area requirement without aisles per workplace:

Ladner:

Assistant with standard desk and tambour roll shutter cupboards	3·9 m²
Assistant with executive desk (1·40 × 0·70 m)	2·0 m²

Schnelle [2, p 30]

    Typewriter workplace $1 \cdot 7$ m²

    Assistant $2 \cdot 3$ m²

    Filing clerk $1 \cdot 9$ m²

    Switchboard operator $2 \cdot 5$ m²

Tiedemann

    Clerical staff $2 \cdot 0$ m²

    Assistant with desk and filing cabinet $6 \cdot 0$ m²

    Assistant with desk and additional appliances $8 \cdot 0$ m²

Boje

    Assistant:

    Desk 156×78 cm $= 1 \cdot 22$ m²

    Moving about area with chair 156×80 cm $= 1 \cdot 25$ m²

    Cupboard area 156×40 cm $= 0 \cdot 62$ m²

    Longitudinal side area 30×198 cm $= 0 \cdot 59$ m²

    Total area 186×198 cm $= 3 \cdot 68$ m²

    Clerical staff:

    Typewriter desk 120×60 cm $= 0 \cdot 72$ m²

    Area for movement with chair 120×70 cm $= 0 \cdot 84$ m²

    Longitudinal side area 30×130 cm $= 0 \cdot 39$ m²

    Total area 150×130 cm $= 1 \cdot 95$ m²

    Technical draughtsman:

    Working table 150×70 cm $= 1 \cdot 05$ m²

    Drawing board portion* 150×25 cm $= 0 \cdot 38$ m²

    Area for movement with chair 150×100 cm $= 1 \cdot 50$ m²

    Total area 150×195 cm $= 2 \cdot 93$ m²

Schmalenbach-Gesellschaft:

    Technical draughtsman with double row

        arrangement:

    L-shape with table for depositing

        equipment $6 \cdot 30$ m²

    L-shape with writing table $7 \cdot 97$ m²

---

* Here the work table is underneath the largest part of the drawing board, so that the latter requires only a fraction of its furniture area as supporting surface area.

Parallel form, drawing equipment and
    writing table   8·26 m²*

U-shape with writing table and table for
    depositing equipment   10·32 m²

2. *Gross area per workplace*

(*a*) General mean values in closed-plan offices

    6 m² per ordinary employee

    9 m² per secretary

    12 m² per senior employee

    18 m² per departmental head

    20 m² per sectional head (director, manager)

(*b*) Various authors

4·5 m²	Office staff in large office	Joedicke
4·5 m²	Ordinary office worker	Connecticut Life Insurance (USA)
4–5 m²	Executive office employee	Rosenkranz
5 m²	Ordinary office staff	Rimpl
6·7 m²	Secretary or technician	Connecticut Life Insurance (USA)
6·0–7·3 m²	Office staff in large office	Riphen (USA)
8 m²	Office staff	DAG
7–12 m²	Office employee	KGVV
7·5–8·5 m²	Employee in double room	Joedicke
9·3 m²	Departmental head, ordinary	Connecticut Life Insurance (USA)
10 m²	Sales clerk (mean)	Rimpl
12 m²	Technical staff (mean)	Rimpl
12 m²	Professional or technical assistant	Schmalenbach-Gesellschaft
13·4 m²	Departmental head, senior	Connecticut Life Insurance (USA)
18·5 m²	2nd Vice-President	Connecticut Life Insurance (USA)
18·0–24.0 m²	Secretariat with 2 secretaries	Schmalenbach-Gesellschaft
18·0 m²	Departmental head without conference table	Schmalenbach-Gesellschaft
20 m²	Senior employee (mean)	Rimpl

* This does not imply that the writing table is pushed underneath the drawing board of the man [1, p 47].

24·0 m²	Departmental head with conference table	Schmalenbach-Gesellschaft
27·9 m²	1st Vice-President	Connecticut Life Insurance (USA)
36·0–42·0 m²	Managing director, Board	Schmalenbach-Gesellschaft

Area comparisons—closed and open plan

Table A2.1 Gross area per workplace

	Closed plan, m²	Open plan, m²
Without fittings and aisles		
Schmalenbach-Gesellschaft	9–10	
Schweins	10	
Siegel:		
Schoolroom arrangement		5–6
Asymmetrical arrangement		8–12
Boje	10·5	9·3
Gottschalk	9–10	10·5
With fittings and aisles		
Schmalenbach-Gesellschaft	17–20	
Boje	21 (mean)	16 (mean)
Rosenkranz	16–17	12
Gottschalk	21–24	17·5

Capital expenditure

Table A2.2 Effective areas

	Closed plan, %		Open plan, %	
	Fittings and aisles	*Effective areas*	*Fittings and aisles*	*Effective areas*
Schmalenbach-Gesellschaft:				
Normal building	31	69		
High building	38	62		
Schweins	30–35	65–70		
Siegel:				
Normal building	40	60		
High building			20–30	70–80
			26 (mean)	74 (mean)
Low building			10–20	80–90
			16 (mean)	84 (mean)
Single-storey building			5	95

Table A2.3 Total building costs

Type of building	Unit	Closed plan, DM	Open plan, DM
Normal building without air-conditioning	Place	15,000–20,000	
Henn:			
High building with air-conditioning	Place		25,000
Low building	Place		12,500
Müller-Lutz and Ladner	Place		9,700–12,500
Ströbel:			
High building	m³		250
Low building	m³		170
Gottschalk			
Up to 5 floors	m³	160–217	177–217
High building (14–20 floors)	m³	230–310	
Up to 5 floors	Place	12,800–17,400	14,000–17,200
high building (14–20 floors)	Place	22,000–30,000	
Boje:			
High building	Place	20,000–45,000	18,000–30,440
Low building	Place	16,000–20,000	11,500–20,000
Most frequent value	Place	25,000	19,000

Part B

CONTRIBUTIONS FROM FIRMS WITH OPEN-PLAN OFFICES

---

edited by Axel Boje

Firm 1

Buch und Ton, Gütersloh

by Kurt H. Schuldes

Our undertaking has lived with the open-plan office now for more than seven years.

1.1 Definition

There is no single opinion as to what an open-plan office really is. In the first place there are many different words for the open-plan office, in our experience. The most common term is 'open-plan office', which is the one we use in our firm, generally shortening it to 'open plan' (literal German: 'area' or 'room').

Another expression is 'open office area', whilst the term 'landscaped office' places emphasis on the layout. Others talk of 'functional office' and a well-known interior designer coined the expression 'room spray' for the landscaped office.

A Sunday paper has called this phenomenon 'the large theatre'. A product-testing journal has paraphrased the term in somewhat dramatic terms as 'Big Brother is watching you'. Still others call the open-plan office 'the ultimate in offices' and even 'office hall'. A well-known American newspaper was defeated by the German invention *Büroland-schaft* (office landscape) and kept the original foreign word in the English. This American paper spoke of a cross between a hotel entrance hall, ship's lounge and airport departure lounge.

1.2 Principles

The following principles are inseparably associated with the landscaped open-plan office:

1 The open area must be of a certain size.
2 Its ground plan differs from that of the conventional office. It

must be technically equipped (with air-conditioning, visual and acoustic fittings, etc.). The open-plan office is designed for all the commercial employees of a concern and embraces all hierarchical levels.

3 The workplaces must be so arranged that the working surfaces of other employees are not directly in one's line of vision. Aisles, distracting machines or glaring windows should not be directly in the line of vision of workplaces.

4 The workplaces should be provided with screens. Aisles through the open-plan office should be free of obstructions; each workplace must have a means of access devoid of obstruction.

5 Machines should not be placed near sound reflectors.

6 The workplaces of executive employees especially should be visually screened.

7 The workplaces of executive employees must be at least 4·5 m away from the next workplace.

8 The workplaces of executive employees may only have one means of access.

9 Aisles should not extend directly behind workplaces. Screens should denote and demarcate regions. The open-plan office should not be able to be fully overlooked.

10 The interviewing corner must be well isolated, in order to avoid disturbance from visitors.

11 There must be inaccessible zones.

12 There must be conference zones.

13 There must be social zones.

1.3 Attitude of the public to the open-plan office

The open-plan office has had a particularly bad press from the public, particularly from those who 'know all about it', i.e. those persons who are to work in an open-plan office one day.

The considerable opposition, which comes somewhere between absolute rejection and silent suffering, has subjective reasons. I have tried to ferret out all the reasons for rejection and list them as follows:

Open plan comes from America.

People do not want to be supervised and watched all the time.

The open-plan office is a continual breeding ground for gossip.

In the open-plan office people are levelled out.

In the open-plan office people are in a mass.

The open-plan office destroys individuality.

In the open-plan office one is noticeable on less hard-working days but one cannot give the same output every day. One is shy of speaking to superiors when every one can see.

A new employee now has 200 critical pairs of eyes on him instead of what used to be 5.

Late comers are conspicuous.

Telephone and personal conversations can be seen and heard by everyone.

Exhibitionists can get the best seats and can show off.

Rest rooms are so arranged that people can be supervised even during breaks.

In the open-plan office there is a greater risk of infection.

Is not rationality an excuse for oppression?

The open-plan office is at best suitable for repetitive work.

Public opinion seems unanimous that the alternative to the open-plan office is obviously the single room.

1.4 Our initial situation

When we acquired the open-plan office in 1961, having informed our employees of these plans during 1960, we had the admitted advantage of not yet having public opinion against us. The reason is obvious—at that time, apart from the open-plan office of C. F. Boehringer (Mannheim), there was as yet no comparable office. On the other hand we lacked the opportunity of showing functional open-plan offices to some of our workers or at least to the executive staff and the Works Council. The arguments advanced at that time against the planning of the open-plan office would nevertheless appear to be substantially the same as those used today by workers having to move into open-plan offices.

The attitudes of the employees were:

In general, opinions ranged from negative to cautious with one positive aspect, a certain curiosity.

The employees feared constant supervision, some in case they lost a cushy job, others, who were overworked, in case they were put under additional pressure from visual and acoustic disturbances.

The employees did not want to sit where they could be seen by everyone; they thought they would not be able to concentrate and were afraid of the unknown.

The feeling of losing individuality and of only being a number in future, was prevalent.

Others saw in the proposed open-plan office the price that had to be paid for shorter working hours, higher salaries and longer leave.

The loss of an intimate atmosphere was bitterly resented: 'You can't blow your nose without 200 people seeing.'

Being compelled to adjust was also resented: There was a fear that private contacts would be lost, and the feeling of always having the boss or even merely an adversary in the office was oppressive.

The attitudes of specialists and executives were:

Executives were particularly critical, their main argument being loss of prestige and the fear of being susceptible to disturbance.

Particular pockets of criticism formed round specialist assistants without actual executive function and also round secretaries and clerks.

1.4.1 Preparatory measures

We knew of these negative attitudes from numerous individual discussions and group conferences. We therefore began, very early, to do everything in our power to enlighten those affected and explain rationally what our idea really was. We held group discussions and with the aid of a model which we had already had made, and which still serves us today for planning conversions and guided visits, we showed how our open-plan office would one day look. The various planning phases of the planning team were scrupulously synchronized with one another.

The planning team consisted of a group of inside specialists, who were supplemented as necessary by outside specialists and architects, and decor, light and noise experts.

Besides the principles already mentioned we drew up some others:

Superiors should sit with their backs to their employees.

The social zone would consist of rest rooms and an expensively fitted out ladies' powder room.

Careful communication counts should determine liability to visual disturbance, in order to reduce it to a minimum by appropriate measures.

All shrill noises should be reduced to a minimum (telephones).

In the circumstances, the most we could do was to negotiate a truce. We told people that they should not immediately throw up the sponge but should wait and see what the open-plan office was really like.

We specifically drew employees' attention to the possibility of their giving notice, which was still open to anyone even after the moving-in date. It should be pointed out that Gütersloh has several industries which at that time were suffering from a considerable labour shortage, so that in fact workers wanting to, could have changed jobs at any time. We simply demanded loyalty of the executive staff and asked them not to negatively influence the workers. We kept the executive staff especially informed and this also applied to members of the Works Council.

I would mention here that I was one of the executive staff who viewed the matter with great scepticism and could not believe in the viability of an open-plan office. The doubter was later converted. I can therefore say from personal experience that the underlying loyalty of executive staff does prevail, if the chief executive stands square and firm behind the firm's objectives.

1.5 Moving in

We took advantage of the only positive motive known to us: curiosity. We spread the move over 14 days, moving one working group after another into the new office.

It is a definite fact that a brand-new open-plan office makes an outstanding impression; it smells freshly of new paint; the new office furniture, the carpet, the plants—everything shines with cleanliness and creates an inviting atmosphere.

What we had expected did in fact happen: those employees who were not yet in the new office, visited their colleagues in their breaks and were, so to speak, greedy to gain their own experience. We did not fail to continue the initial group discussions even after the move, at intervals of one, two and three months. We soon found to our own astonishment that the serious anti-open-plan arguments had evaporated. As human beings must apparently always have a reason to grumble about something, we heard fresh arguments, but these did not carry any real weight and were not likely to make the project fail.

Such arguments were: 'The plants smell—there is a draught from the air-conditioning plant in some places—one's voice sounds unnatural— what price will we now have to pay for being presented with such an office?'

Without any doubt we managed to stand up to the changeover very well. Now, after more than seven years' activity in the open-plan office, everything has returned to normal, enthusiasm has subsided just as the negative arguments have disappeared.

1.6 Experiences

1.6.1 Increase in output

The experiences we have had with our open-plan office have been overwhelmingly positive. In the first place we have recorded a considerable rise in output since 1961. As, however, from the date of moving into the open-plan office, we modified some of our methods, we cannot now say with certainty what proportion of the 40 per cent output increase is attributable to the changed work methods and what proportion to the open-plan office. But we have no doubt in our own minds that the open-plan office has produced an improvement in output. Departments in which no changes were made in work methods can now manage with less staff than before or have taken on additional functions; I am thinking for example of my own sphere, personnel management.

1.6.2 Information and communication

Information flow is much smoother. Memoranda have almost completely stopped; telephone conversations are largely replaced by personal contact with other people. The decline in cliquishness is quite remarkable.

We have ascertained that in the open-plan office each employee has a large number of contacts, but individual contacts are impersonal and superficial. This may be disadvantageous to sensitive employees, but is undoubtedly an advantage to the firm.

1.6.3 Flexibility

Possibilities for making changes in work flow, setting up new working groups and extending old ones, do not require expensive conversions and structural alterations. A conversion of approximately 15 workplaces for example, which we carried out one week-end, cost us one working day for three employees in the organization and methods department for the planning work and the conversion was then carried out within two hours of knocking-off time, having already been effected on a model.

1.6.4 Social atmosphere

We think that the working atmosphere in our open-plan office is apparent. The relationships between superiors, between superiors and subordinates and between the workers as a whole have considerably improved. Manners have become much better.

The open-plan office automatically does away with shouting bosses, or even those who merely raise their voices. The environmental conditions affecting every employee at his desk are therefore good or at least acceptable. Acoustic stresses, which were so feared, are far less when compared with conventional offices.

Mutual training of the employees in consideration and respect for one another is gratifying. In this respect we mean social training rather than superimposed discipline. Status symbols are not very prevalent in our open-plan office. They are restricted to special visual screening of the workplaces of executive staff and to a different wood for the desks and filing cabinets (teak). We would today have no difficulty in eliminating the status symbol of a different desk completely.

In the interval every employee has come to know who's who and does not need to be visually reminded. Initially, however, it would not have been possible to do away with status symbols for those senior staff, who exist in our firm as in any other, who feel a great need for prestige.

We have ascertained that our open-plan office was considerably cheaper than conventional design would have been. In the open-plan office people work harder and more concentratedly and we find that a consolidation of output is noticeable at every desk. Last, but not least, one must mention the civilized atmosphere and lack of affectation in dealings with subordinates and with one another. One or two pleasing side-effects of the open-plan office have been observed. Formal greetings have virtually disappeared and a brief 'Good morning' and nod is considered sufficient.

1.6.5 Breaks

The rest rooms have become an accepted and popular institution. At first there were difficulties because they became overcrowded at certain break periods, mainly between 8.30 and 10 am. Now breaks are evenly distributed over the whole working day and although the frequency and duration of breaks is left to individual judgement, we have recorded average coffee breaks morning and afternoon of 18 minutes each. The fact that anyone can visit the rest room whenever he wants to, reduces so-called arbitrary breaks, which in any case are, in our experience, far more frequent in conventional offices.

1.6.6 Disturbances

It is an interesting fact that scarcely any employee looks up when someone passes his workplace. This discovery always surprises our visitors. Of course visitors in the public limelight are an exception. Such visitors as Chris Howland, Willy Brandt, Renate Holm, etc., are announced beforehand, so that the employees can for once see something of the outside world as well. The interest that the press, radio, television and documentary film world have shown in open-plan offices has met with approval from our workers: they feel interesting and noticed. The open-plan office is a constant source of communication stimulus.

When I, for example, am walking through the office, I usually make between three and five visits to different workplaces and thus save myself a host of intended conferences and appointments. The same goes for all the executive staff in this office. On the other hand, it must be said that the enjoyment of contact in the open-plan office can also become a burden, if the possibility of easy communication becomes too much of a temptation to the employees. In this case steps must be taken to ensure that executives at least can have undesirable visitors intercepted by a secretary located in the only path of access. In any case susceptibility to disturbance varies from individual to individual.

There are people who, on principle, never look up from their work. It does not matter to such persons if a visitor is standing and looking at him from about four to five metres away. Others become aware of such contact signals immediately and these can in themselves constitute a disturbance. Individual workplaces must therefore be appropriately screened according to the type of employee—I am talking now of executives.

The main body of employees, once they have had time to get used to it, behave in a manner befitting the open-plan office. It is considered rude to interrupt a person who is concentrating hard on his work and it is not the done thing to make contact if the person concerned already has visitors.

One must, however, expect the so-called 'open-plan nuisances'. These are workers who will not take a friendly hint, and permit themselves to interrupt the work of colleagues at any time of the day. In time this also improves, although repeated hints must be given. Quite definitely, behaviour has improved and so has dress. The improvement in style of dress is particularly noticeable in departments having a predominantly female element and is of great importance. Apparently our ladies derive pleasure from showing off their new spring costumes and do not hesitate to do so.

1.6.7 Noise

We have assembled all office machines which cause considerable noise (typewriters for example) at one central point, a so-called sound zone. This was not so at the beginning, but the flexibility of the office made such a change readily possible.

Also in the course of the years we have created management zones in which, contrary to the original conception, we have accommodated all main departmental heads, not with their departments but where their need for communication is greatest, i.e. next to one another. This means that the sectional heads sit relatively close to one another, regardless of where their workers are. Experience has proved that communication between main departmental heads is more frequent than 'from above downwards'.

Too much quiet in the open-plan office is just as undesirable as too much noise. We notice this very clearly when, after knocking-off time for example, the main body of employees has left the room and there are only a few persons left. In such an atmosphere individual noises are perceptible over long distances and confidential discussions are no longer possible. As our phon level is normally between 45 and 55, the average noise stress is low, again in comparison with conventional offices.

We have discovered that most of our employees feel upgraded by the relatively luxurious furnishing of the open-plan office. A good example of this is our punched card operators, who were for a long time accommodated in our open-plan office and then for organizational reasons had to be removed to a conventional punched card room in another part of the firm. There was immediate unrest amongst these operators and they tried with all their might to get back into the open-plan office. It is worthy of note that many workers feel hemmed in in smaller office rooms, in which they have occasional business. The stimulus of being surrounded by a working atmosphere is lacking—the walls are too close. We initially created a concentration zone, i.e. screened-off single workplaces in such a manner as to promote absolutely concentrated work. We now notice that the two remaining concentration workplaces are not frequented at all, and we are soon going to get rid of them. The open-plan office has an air of impersonality without being cold. This rationalizes the atmosphere without constricting individuals. It is a striking fact that 'office clown' types who are to be found in every office, fade into insignificance in the open-plan office.

There is no evidence that one has less fun and enjoyment in the open-plan office than in smaller offices. But jokes are less disturbing, they spread over the whole of the office and are moderated. We are frequently asked by visitors what type of person is most suited to open-plan offices. We are now of the opinion that in principle any type of office worker is suited to the open-plan office, as long he does not think himself more important than he really is. The ideal types for the open-plan office are workers who have self-confidence and contentment and consider their job more as a means to an end than as the absolute centre of their existence*.

The old type employee, the book-keeper for example who is married to his books or the cashier who has become part of his cash-desk, the type that has never been eager for contact, is less willing to occupy an open-plan office. But there is today no question that he can.

* This is the author's personal opinion.

1.6.8 Room fitting

Technical niceties of furnishing in our experience play a less significant role in the open-plan office than is commonly supposed. Our chairs are an example of this. We have chairs with adjustable backs, seating equipment with which specialists took an extraordinary amount of trouble to see that they were anatomically sound and beneficial to health. Six months ago we noticed by chance that very few of our workers even knew that the backs were adjustable, although there is a clear notice to this effect on the back of the chair. For some reason or other we had forgotten to refer to this in our 'open-plan office instructions'. The adjustable back simply went unnoticed although we had taken so much trouble. It was also interesting to note that the redecoration of our open-plan office, including recovering of our screens, which we carried out $3\frac{1}{2}$ years ago, scarcely aroused any response in our employees. The freshening up of the office cost us approximately DM 80,000. We had to ask for our workers' opinions formally, and then what came to light was not very instructive.

It will perhaps be said that the occupants of an open-plan office are visually insensitive, but it may merely be that even bold colour combinations, whilst arousing a certain interest, are not perceived as a discussion-worthy change.

New employees to the firm settle down in the open-plan office in about 14 days. It is confirmed by all new workers that they are far less conspicuous in the first few days than in conventional offices and this makes the settling down period much easier for them.

1.7   Executive staff in the open-plan office

It is interesting to note that the fact (so frequently criticized at the beginning) of the boss sitting in the same room as a constant supervising element, is today no longer discussed. Whereas in conventional offices a visit from a superior is felt to be a check-up, the fact that several bosses are always there nowadays ensures that the presence of superiors is not felt to be supervision, even if in fact it is so. Exactly the opposite of what was feared has occurred for it is not the worker who is in a glass case under everyone's critical eye, but the boss who is the focal point of his own workers. If he is self-confident and enjoys responsibility, this does not worry him. We would even say that the awareness of having constantly to prove himself in front of his own workers, counts among his obligations as an executive.

H   99

The open-plan office compels frankness and thereby influences the general style of management.

Supervision of workers is, contrary to initial fears, neither more nor less than in conventional offices.

We have observed that appreciation of the work problems of others has increased.

The position of the superior undergoes a certain mutation in the open-plan office. He is respected by his employees working in the same room for his personality or ability, and no longer just because he is the boss. In this respect the open-plan office demands a great deal from its management team.

1.7.1 Position of the secretary

In the open-plan office the secretary's position is weakened, because now that she no longer sits in a single room, she has no opportunity of wielding her power, for example by giving certain visitors preferential treatment over others.

As we found that typewriters are better accommodated in a noise zone, we centralized the entire typing services in a so-called central secretariat and relieved the secretary proper of typing duties.

We utilized the released capacity by having one secretary for two and in one case even for three departmental heads. Altogether we made a 50 per cent saving in secretaries.

It is obvious that loss of power is one of the main reasons for the opposition which secretaries in particular raise to the open-plan idea.

It is interesting to note that workers who occasionally grumble or have something to criticize about the open-plan office amongst themselves, defend this conception outside the office—that is, once they have become convinced of the advantages of the open-plan office or at least have come to see things rationally.

Another remarkable fact is the lack of amorous pre-occupations in the open-plan office.

1.8 Disadvantages

The following disadvantages are of importance in open-plan office planning:

1 It seems well-nigh impossible to install a satisfactorily functioning air-conditioning plant. It is always a source of annoyance and

fraying tempers. There is the additional factor that the blame for intolerably hot weather is apparently laid not on the season, e.g. dog-days, but on the open-plan office or the air-conditioning plant.

2 As soon as the office is occupied and the workers have gathered their first experiences, an initial lowering of standards of discipline is noticed.

3 The desire to regain independence provokes shifting of screens to suit individual wishes, the bringing of souvenirs, putting up of holiday postcards, etc., and an obvious tendency to disorder. By continual education in the common interest, such tendencies should be politely but firmly resisted.

4 Plain desks—the furniture must, of course, be in keeping with the open-plan office—arouse very different responses. We had some difficulties with these.

5 Bars on the use of the telephone at certain times or other general regulations of this nature are very difficult to put into practice in the open-plan office and with us at any rate they have not been successful.

6 The open-plan office is disadvantageous in special situations, such as the death of an employee during working hours, during a particularly critical political situation or in the case of a nervous breakdown.

7 As soon as an open-plan office is set up, there appear members of all the institutions which want to investigate 'open-plan persons' for experimental purposes. Sociology students in particular, all types of social critics, journalists, etc., are always searching for the ideal field of experiment. There then follow questionnaires, which confuse the ordinary worker rather than serve any useful purpose to anyone. All these also cause disturbances and time losses.

1.9 Recommendations

The following recommendations are the results of our experiences and we shall take them into account in any new office buildings, which will without doubt be of open-plan design:

1 The planning of an open-plan office without the unreserved support of the management or administration is doomed to failure from the start. No office planner, however good, can fight on two fronts.

2 Prompt and thorough notification of all employees affected, including executive staff, is, of course, necessary but it should not take the form of endless debates, which finally increase resistance rather than lessen it.

3 Special treatment in the sense of particularly detailed information, and perhaps an inspection trip, is advisable for particularly obstinate critics. Nevertheless such special treatment should not be clearly manifested as such, because otherwise this group will consider themselves more highly regarded than the others, who really deserve it. Such special treatment must be planned very carefully and be very deliberately thought about.

4 Superiors who in spite of the loyalty expected from them, influence the workers under them against the open-plan office, should be dismissed or otherwise suitably and strictly dealt with. The first instance of such a measure will guarantee peace and quiet for the future.

5 Die-hard objectors must be dismissed because of the disturbance to the peace of the firm. No worker is so valuable that he can be allowed to seriously disturb a great concept. Here again gentle force must be used if necessary—a mode of treatment which has apparently become more and more foreign to us in the last few years.

Nino, Nordhorn

by Dr H. Rodius

2.1 Planning

Our motive for constructing a new office building was shortage of space. We were in a position to erect a *new* building and not just to set up open-plan offices in an existing building. We needed to accommodate 450 to 500 employees. The rough planning for the new administrative building began at the end of 1957. The idea, absolutely revolutionary at that time, of building an office block with open areas each extending over one storey, met a very positive response from our management.

The building with the carefully thought-out ground plan of an irregular octagon, has four upper storeys, a ground floor and basement.

When an office building is being planned, one must first of all be clear about the dimensions: length, breadth and floor area of each storey. Sometimes one is restricted by the existing site. After it has been made clear which departments of the undertaking are to be housed in the new building, one has to find out which is the largest single organizational unit that must be accommodated on one floor and whether and which further departments may perhaps be included on this floor, because they have a close functional connection with this largest unit. One ascertains how many workers there are in these departments, who thus have to be accommodated on one floor, plans a workplace reserve and then multiplies the number of these workers plus reserve by a chosen unit of workplace area which should include access area. This gives the floor area to be occupied by one storey. This measurement then determines the area of the remaining storeys, to which the other departments have to be allocated from the standpoints of function and co-operation.

When calculating the floor areas, however, one must allow extra space for the workplaces of senior employees and for workplaces having an additional space requirement for technical reasons, because such additional requirements are not as a rule uniformly distributed over all

103

floors. The workplace reserve, the percentage of reserve workplaces to the total number of workplaces, depends on the policy of the firm. Do the management intend to expand on the site where the proposed building is to be erected and if so to what foreseeable extent, or is any expansion to be carried out elsewhere? When calculating the reserve workplaces one must not make the mistake of assuming that any increase in workplaces over the present position will in future be equally distributed over all floors. It may very well be that workplaces added in the future will be very disproportionately distributed on each floor, i.e. that only certain departments will become larger and use up the reserve, so that suddenly there is a shortage of space on one floor while perhaps on other floors the reserve is never needed. The reserve must therefore be large enough to accommodate the extra staff of even such disproportionate expansions. Furthermore the number of floors should be as low as possible for reasons of communication, i.e. they should extend horizontally as far as possible and departments having heavy visitor traffic should as far as possible be put on the lower floors.

2.1.1 Planning team

These questions and the numerous other constructional, technical, organizational and psychological questions which arise when planning an open-plan office building, were talked over and decided by a planning team formed for this purpose. This team consisted of the purchasing director, who at the same time acted as secretary for the building project, the organization and methods officer, the leading technical staff of the firm, who had knowledge of lighting and air-conditioning, the firm's psychologist, the architect and the staff of a consultancy firm. This team met about twice a week during the first weeks of planning and the initial stage of building, and somewhat less often as the work progressed.

2.1.2 Psychological preparation

Apart from the technical and organizational problems, one must not neglect to bring one's employees over to the idea of an open-plan office as early as possible. The planning team therefore took employees' representatives on the Works Council with some heads of departments to be accommodated in the administrative building, on visits to the few open-plan examples existing or in the course of erection at the time. After these visits the firm's psychologist and the O & M officer assembled all the staff who were to move into the new block in groups of 20–25 men and women and said to them:

> 'You know, of course, that we are intending to build an open-plan block. Some of us have inspected such open-plan offices but unfortunately we could not take all the firm's employees. We who have seen these offices have gained a very positive impression. But as you were not there, you have no idea what such an office is really like and what it is like to work in one. We would like to tell you about it.'

We then tried during these discussions with our workers to ferret out opinions and questions, and by answering these questions, to give our colleagues a picture of the open-plan office.

2.2 Fitting out

We proceeded similarly in planning the fitting out.

We first determined the individual furniture requirement for each workplace by examining the old workplaces. We then fixed the zones for individual departments and groups on each floor according to workplace requirements and the functional relationship between groups and within groups. This zone distribution, the workplace layout and the furniture arrangement for each floor were then drawn as a plan. At the same time small models of furniture were made out of wood and cardboard by our joinery department. These model desks, cupboards and chairs were then laid out on a large table top, floor by floor according to the plan and the employees were then brought to the table in departments and were told: 'This, ladies and gentlemen, is how the office is to be fitted out. That is your group and this is yours. That is where you sit, and you sit there. Please have a look and give us your opinion.' Everybody was wildly enthusiastic and made all kinds of suggestions for distribution and arrangement of workplaces, and we tried to put these into practice where feasible.

This *psychological preparation* of employees with *prompt information* about building project and the detailed design is very important. It must under no circumstances be forgotten when planning open-plan offices, which to most workers are something new and strange. The outcome is that the workers feel that they have participated in the planning and building and have not been 'passed over'. All this was a great help to us later when moving into the new open-plan building. Everyone moved into the building without built-in resistance, many even with enthusiasm, and this thorough psychological preparation has certainly contributed to the fact that the verdict on the open-plan offices amongst our workers is almost unanimously favourable.

2.3 Building data

Building commenced in October 1961 and the move took place on 1 July 1963. The building is 65 m long, 37 m wide at the widest point and 24 m at the narrowest. The total area of the building is 8,600 m² per storey (without core and supports) and the floor area is 1,300 m². There are about 100 workplaces on each floor. The volume built round is about 38,000 m³. Building costs per cubic metre, i.e. total building costs including external spaces and auxiliary costs, amounted to DM 150, and the building costs per workplace about DM 11,500. The total building costs were DM 5·7 million, with an additional DM 600,000 fitting-out costs.

2.4 Reasons for the open-plan conception

We decided on open-plan offices:

1 Because we see in the open-plan office an adequate expression of sociological and office planning needs in a modern industrial administration. The profusion of information and the increase and variety in functions which are today demanded of any undertaking, lead to ever greater specialization of staff. Specialization demands team work in order to clarify problems and prepare the ground for decisions. Purely external attributes of hierarchical differences in rank, such as single rooms, therefore become questionable. The authority of superiors should rest on personality and performance and not on status symbols.

2 Because we consider the open office more favourable costs-wise than the conventional solution.

3 Because a simple logical consideration speaks in favour of the open-plan office. As far as susceptibility to disturbance is concerned, placing people singly in offices is certainly the most favourable solution, but this is impossible. The usual office in which two, three,

or even five and more employees are accommodated, is however just as certainly the most unfavourable solution as regards disturbance conditions. Ergo—the modern well-designed open-plan office, equipped with all technically possible means of lessening acoustic and even visual disturbances.

When beginning planning we gave our architect the task of comparing the costs of a conventional office building with the costs of an open-plan building of the same capacity. The building costs of an open-plan solution are, in spite of the expensive air-conditioning plant, generally lower than the building costs of a conventional block. But there are also considerable savings even *after* erection of the building, because of the elimination of the costs, which experience has shown to be very high, which are increasingly incurred in conventional office buildings by subsequent erection and removal of partition walls, as soon as organizational changes require it. Also not inconsiderable, although difficult to assess quantitatively, are the savings in operating costs achieved through more fluid inter-communication of persons and things in the open-plan office.

A further improvement achieved by the open-plan office is the lowering of noise level, with good sound-absorbing equipment [44].

2.4.1 New furniture

We decided at that time to acquire new furniture and not take the old furniture into the new building. The choice of a working desk had priority. We decided to develop a desk from our own design. The desk, designed jointly by the O & M man and the architect, consists merely of a table top of wood with four steel legs and a narrow drawer for pencils, erasers and the like. The desk has the usual measurements, 156 × 78 cm, but is only 75 cm high. There are a number of workplaces where we have used this standard desk, but with one pedestal unit. Only four or five employees, including the accountant in the finance division, have a desk with two pedestal units, for easy access to the accounts cards. Papers are as a rule kept not in the desk, but next to it in a movable cabinet, at knee height in suspended files and loose-leaf folders. The desk without pedestal units has the additional advantage that its price is much more favourable than the usual desk with two pedestals. The cabinet-making work for the latter, of course, makes the desk more expensive.

Besides the writing desk our furniture consists of a typing desk, slightly lower and smaller in format, with one pedestal to hold typing paper, and a machine table as long as one narrow side of the writing desk to take calculating machines or typewriters which are only used occasionally. The equipment also includes a steel cabinet having the same height as the writing desk, which is placed at a workplace when a filing cabinet is required. We have also had to erect some 1·40-m high cabinets, to hold departmental records. Finally there are the movable screens, which are also 1·40 m high and the plant troughs. An important aesthetic aspect in the open-plan office is to have as few differences as possible in furniture height and to keep the planes constant.

2.4.2 Flooring

A deep-pile Perlon carpet was used as floor covering. To keep the sound-absorbing properties as effective as possible, a soft pile and not a hard fibre carpet should be used. The floor covering is a deciding factor in an open-plan office. An effective open-plan office without textile floor covering is unthinkable. As the colour of the floor covering also determines the impression given by an open-plan office, the choice of colour was very important to us. We let ourselves be advised by a colour psychologist, because the colours of the work atmosphere, apart from purely aesthetic considerations, are undoubtedly of psychological importance.

Only a light colour wood would tone with the blue of the floor covering, preferably ash. Ash—with the desk tops coated with a matt, transparent polyester—is therefore the colour of all our furniture. The particular shade of the flooring colour must also be matched to the colour of the artificial light and the green of the plants. Our experiments showed that a cobalt blue with a hint of red best satisfied all aesthetic requirements.

The strong, emphatic blue of the flooring, which strikes every visitor, still shocks us a little, even though we have had years to get used to it, although we may be scarcely conscious of it. It is a known fact that the absolutely uniform temperature of the conditioned air that we breathe in the open-plan office has a certain tiring effect towards the end of the working period. It would seem that in order to feel enlivened, human beings need graduated stimuli to their senses. In the open air the different atmospheric stimuli that affect our temperature sense have an invigorating effect on us. We believe that a colour so decisive in the impression made by the room, such as the strong blue of the flooring, affects the sense of sight in a particular way and can to some extent compensate for the lack of stimulus to our temperature sense caused by the constancy of temperature in an air-conditioned office.

2.5 New style of management

The workplaces of executives who are also accommodated in the open-plan office, are, in our firm, fitted out in the same way as the workplaces of the rest of the staff. They therefore differ very little from those of the other employees. The swivel office stool is replaced by a swivel chair. Our justification for this is that the senior man does in fact have to think more than his subordinates and may therefore be allowed the luxury of a more comfortable seat. Secondly the workplace area of the executive is greater than that of the other employees, because it contains in addition to the executive desk, a conference table and chairs for internal discussions. We are of the opinion that the past, distance-emphasizing, more authoritarian and hierarchical style of management, is out of date, and in firms that keep pace with the requirements of our time, has long been replaced by a form of guidance of a more informa-tive and co-operative nature. The decisions which today have to be made by management in a business world of complicated and different-iated circumstances, are more difficult than ever before. Less than ever can they rest on solitary or intuitive resolutions, however precise. They require very thorough preparation by those who have the necessary detailed knowledge at their finger-tips. Such decisions are nowadays generally reached by teams, which are either in permanent existence for certain types of problem or are formed *ad hoc*. In these teams or committees employees from very different hierarchical levels may be represented, according to their experience and specialized knowledge. Because of this all-embracing and intensive co-operation between employees having different positions in the firm, which today is a simple matter of necessity, the inter-personal relations between executive and non-executive have also undergone a change. They have, through force of circumstances, been rationalized. The changes in style of manage-ment and in work methods mean that the director or executive can no longer wield his authority simply by virtue of his position in the firm's hierarchy. He must derive his authority from his own personality and the quality of his work. This means, however, that external status symbols which were formerly so stressed (single rooms, outer rooms, expensive furniture and the like) become much less significant. He who achieves something, *is* somebody, even without badges of rank. In any event we have had no difficulty in placing even executives in the open-plan office and fitting out their workplaces in the same way as all the others—apart from the two differences mentioned above. These two single differences in workplaces (chair instead of stool and larger workplace area) are rationally motivated. At the same time, however, they may serve as 'signs of rank' to satisfy any prestige needs still prevalent.

2.6 The move

The move into the new building was no problem. At the time of the move the furniture and equipment were in their pre-arranged places. The desks had names on them so that everyone knew where his place in the building was. The open-plan office was accepted, not least because of the psychological preparation. The reactions were perhaps also positive because previous offices had in some cases been too small or because something new arouses interest.

2.7 Air-conditioning plant

In the more than five years that we have so far spent in the open-plan office, very valuable experience has been obtained. Scarcely one of the employees has taken an absolutely negative attitude to the new office. This does not mean to say, however, that voices have not been raised in criticism. But this criticism is not so much directed against the open-plan office as such, but against certain concomitant phenomena, which are easily remedied. If, say, the air-conditioning plant is not functioning as it should, and this does sometimes happen, people are quick to lay the blame not on the plant but on the open-plan office. The latter is thus identified with the air-conditioning plant. Some employees, apparently particularly sensitive in this regard, complained at times very indignantly about the office because the air did not contain enough oxygen and they therefore felt exhausted. We immediately asked the air-conditioning experts about this and they proved quite definitely that the requirements set down on this point in the DIN regulations for air-conditioning plants, were more than fulfilled by our plant and it was impossible for the air not to contain enough oxygen. We told our employees this, but the complaints were repeated from time to time, until we found out that they were justified, in so far as the cause of the discomfort, although not lack of oxygen, was occasional insufficiency of moisture content. This was the case in winter, when the weather outside was cold and frosty. This very dry outside air was then heated in the air-conditioning chambers but not sufficiently moisturized. An additional appliance has since been incorporated to remedy this defect.

The lighting programme in the open-plan office presents no difficulties in the face of modern lighting techniques. The acoustic factors, however, are more important.

2.8 Noise in the open-plan office

Causes of noise disturbance in the open-plan office can usually be eliminated. Such sources of noise are, for example, particularly noisy machines or just people who speak loudly. Fortunately the environmental influence of the open-plan office is generally so effective that in the course of time even such persons tone down their powerful voices. When, nevertheless, we occasionally have cause to complain, the offenders are usually employees who often travel on business, and in the office retain their usual outside voices.

Such workers—and likewise any disturbing office machines—can be placed away from the rest of the staff. The intensity of sound decreases with increasing distance from the source and the greater the sound-absorption in the room the greater the decrease. This is achieved by sound-deadening ceilings, textile floor-covering or half-size screens. The decisive factor in overcoming acoustic problems in the open-plan office, however, is always the general noise level produced by the sum of all single noises (conversations, telephones, office machines) and is dependent on the number of employees and office machines in the room.

2.9 Output in the open-plan office

During the many visits we receive, the following questions are always asked. What is output like in the open-plan office? Is it greater or smaller than in a conventional office? What influence does the open-plan office have on staff turnover? What about sickness quota? Do you have difficulty in getting staff when they learn that they are to work in an open-plan office?

We have not carried out any investigations into these aspects or made any measurements, as far as these can be made. But we have been able to observe that in no way is output in the open-plan office lower, or absenteeism and sickness greater than in a conventional office. The contrary is rather the case. In our experience applicants for jobs consider our open-plan office an attractive feature. Only in a very few cases have we had difficulties. There have been for example two cases of secretaries who could only conceive of working in an outer office, and whose services we therefore had to dispense with. Applicants for the post of draughtsman have also occasionally entertained doubts as to whether they would feel happy in the drawing office zone of our open-plan office. On the other hand we can also quote examples where employment begun with us for a period fixed by the employee has automatically been extended, the reason given for the extension of contract being that the atmosphere of the open-plan office particularly appeals to the employee.

2.9.1 Confidential discussions

Another question which is often asked—Can confidential conversations be readily conducted in the open plan office? Yes—if the place in which they take place (and possibly workplaces of personnel assistants also) are at a sufficient distance from the others.

The open-plan office does not create any difficulties in interviews with clients. When planning our office building we were rather doubtful at first whether the necessary privacy of conversations with clients could be ensured, if the interview was to take place in the open-plan office in an interviewing cubicle merely separated by screens, when there might be a discussion taking place with a competitor of this client in the adjacent cubicle. We have found out, however, that the general noise level and sound absorption are quite sufficient to render the content of the conversation in the adjacent cubicles unintelligible. We have merely increased the height of the $1 \cdot 40$ m screens to $1 \cdot 80$ m in the visitors' cubicles in order to add visual screening to the sound-proofing effect.

2.9.2 Mental concentration

Another frequent question—Can one work concentratedly in an open-plan office? People obviously vary greatly in their powers of concentration. But here again experience shows that a workplace in an open-plan office does allow concentrated mental activity, although one or two senior employees may perhaps find concentration easier if their workplaces are enclosed by visual screens. Even extroverts, the type of worker whose powers of concentration are such that he is distracted more easily than others by happenings around him, and who one would assume would find it particularly hard in an open-plan office, soon accustom themselves to the particular working conditions of this type of office. Even they scarcely look up when, say, a group of visitors is being shown round the building.

2.9.3 Sociological group consciousness

One very positive factor in favour of the open-plan office is that the individual gains a much greater awareness of the value of his own work than when this work is performed in isolation or with only a few colleagues. He experiences the collective achievement of an entire undertaking much more visibly and intensively in the open-plan office and is thus more conscious of the fact that even his own small cog is essential to the turning of the wheels of the firm. And, likewise, the open-plan office demonstrates to the worker very clearly that other departments also have a necessary part to play in the general scheme of things. Appreciation of the work of colleagues thus also increases; cliques do not flourish in the open-plan office.

The atmosphere of the open-plan office also encourages the formation of what psychologists and sociologists call 'informal groups', that is inter-personal relations extending beyond organizational group boundaries, by virtue of common outlooks, interests or likes and dislikes. One should in no way underestimate the importance to working life of the human contacts which are particularly furthered by the open-plan office—think of rest rooms for example. The ability to make diverse and easy contact is to many persons a necessary condition of feeling at home in their working environment. This applies particularly to young people, young girls especially, who have to work away from home. They find it particularly gratifying that relations with their male and female colleagues, including work groups other than their own, are facilitated by the open-plan office.

2.9.4 Flexibility and communication

Finally a few remarks as to the extent to which the open-plan office contributes to the rationalization of administration. On this point I can be very brief. The advantages of the open-plan offices are obvious. In connection with costs I have already spoken of the very decisive factor of the flexibility of a one-floor office in all organizational alterations involving shifting of workplaces. The easy re-arrangement, increasing or reducing of workplaces in the room, without having to move built-in partitions, is the most striking advantage of the open-plan office. It is self-evident that the larger the room itself, the greater is this mobility within the room, an argument which—in addition to acoustic demands (sound reflection)—favours such areas being made as large as possible. There is also the saving in time and money through the easier inter-communication of persons and the less lengthy transport of papers and the like in the open-plan office. Such savings are again not easily measured but they are clearly quite considerable.

2.10 Summary

The open-plan office is the office of the future. Nevertheless it does also have its problems which must be looked at critically and in some cases are difficult to overcome. Experience shows, however, that a well-designed open-plan office which is really worthy of the name by virtue of its dimensions, technical equipment and fittings, is far superior to conventional office solutions: superior from the viewpoint of organizational work management, from the important psychological and sociological aspects and not least from the costs point of view.

By our definition, however, open-plan offices are only practicable in the future for those concerns that can put a sufficient number of staff in areas of sufficient dimensions. In our opinion an open-plan office is functional only if it covers at least 400 m² and the distance from wall to wall is at least 20 m. It has meanwhile become common knowledge that the modern open-plan area, for which unfortunately no really appropriate name has yet been found, is not simply an enlarged office room. One should not therefore blame the genuine open-plan office for the disadvantages that a 'large office' has.

Unfortunately there are also open-plan offices which do not come up to expectations. The reason for this can only be that such offices have been inadequately planned, and set up in ignorance of the prerequisites for an open-plan office.

Planning in this still very new field creates problems beyond those of a purely technical building nature, which cannot be solved immediately. One should therefore devote great care to planning and draw on the experience acquired in the good open-plan offices now in existence.

Part C

SYMPOSIUM

---

edited by Axel Boje

Open-plan and conventional offices for optional use

by Gerhard Balser

GERHARD BALSER ARCHITECTURAL ORGANISATION,
FRANKFURT AM MAIN

1.1 Introduction

Many builders deciding to build open-plan office premises would like to reserve the possibility of dividing these up again into conventional offices at any time. They want the recognized advantages of flexibility to remain in that the partitions must be able to be changed around at any time without great expense, when new circumstances require it.

The necessary expenditure is very rarely known. Added to this is the fact that the capital investment required is often doubtful because open-plan offices require quite different constructional units and technical equipment from conventional offices and are not created by simply omitting the partition walls in a normal office building. The specific characteristics of both types of building are too different.

This starts right from the dimensions. The size and shape of an open-plan office are, apart from the requirements of a free arrangement of furniture, determined by acoustics. The noise level in rooms whose walls are less than 20 m apart is too high, because sound is reflected from one window wall to the other. The lowest limit for the dimensions of a good open-plan office is therefore 20 × 20 m.

1.2 Air-conditioning

A room of this size must be air-conditioned, because natural ventilation is no longer possible in a room of this depth. It is generally carried out by two separate plants for the outer and inner zones.

Whilst the plant for the outer zone requires complicated technical equipment and regulation, in order to convert the constantly changing external influences into a uniform room atmosphere, the plant for the inner zone has to only fulfil constant conditions year in, year out, namely blow in fresh air and conduct away body heat and that generated by lights, and is therefore much less complicated.

It is not difficult to see that the greater the proportion of inner zone to outer zone and the smaller the proportion of window area as an influencing factor in the outer zone, the simpler and cheaper is the air-conditioning.

The technical conditions of an open-plan office are therefore always more favourable, the deeper and more compact the office area is.

A conventional office building with rational ground plan is 12–15 m wide. It can only be extended lengthways and upwards.

If one wishes an open-plan office to be used later in conventional layout, the utilization of a room at least 20 m deep is scarcely possible, unless one puts enclosed record offices, conference rooms, etc., in the central zone in a triple arrangement. But even the provision of conference rooms, which have a relatively high number of persons in relation to floor area, is as a rule not possible without additional air-conditioning measures, whilst the existing air-conditioning plant is much too expensive for record rooms.

At best, therefore, one has a triple layout administrative building, the degree of utilization of which compares most unfavourably with conventional administrative buildings, and the air-conditioning plant of which, conceived for open-plan requirements, is uneconomic. In order, however, to be usable at all after conversion, the piping for the open-plan solution must be considerably more expensive than would have been necessary, in order that later every possible single room can have a suitable inlet and outlet of air. At the same time the ducts must be so arranged that telephone connections from one room to another are not obstructed. If it is desired that the occupants of the single rooms should be able to regulate the air-conditioning individually—and this is advisable for personal comfort—this facility must be provided from the beginning. In the open-plan office, however, it is undesirable.

Thus in the initial open-plan solution additional measures have to be incorporated in the central controls, in the duct and piping network and in the regulating means, which even then do not guarantee a good solution after subdivision into single rooms.

The smaller the axes for possible partition walls, the greater is the extra expenditure on air-conditioning plant.

1.3 Sectional partitions

If the partitions in conventionally subdivided premises are required to be changed round at any time without great expense, they must be clamped between floor and ceiling. If tolerably adequate sound-proofing is expected of such partitions, this will make them extremely expensive. Additional arrangements also have to be made, to prevent the transmission of sound over the partition through the hollow space above the suspended ceiling.

Thus, for example, partition mountings could be included right from the beginning in all the longitudinal and transverse axes concerned. This would be a considerable expense in a conventional office; in an open-plan office it seems absurd.

However, mountings could also be incorporated above the walls at the time of erecting the partitions. But this again considerably restricts flexibility.

1.4 Sound-proofing

Another possibility is a sound-proofed construction of the suspended ceiling, so that the rooms are self-contained. This means, however, that the ceiling is thick and heavy and therefore expensive, and even built-in lights have to have a sound-proof lining, and all the waste air must be passed into ducts as soon as it leaves the room.

A quite considerable expense is therefore necessitated in the ceiling construction to provide for the eventuality of later sub-division, which is unnecessary during use as an open-plan office.

There are also different limits on the noise level of an air-conditioning plant in open-plan and single offices. The DIN level of 45 phon in the open-plan office is too loud after sub-division into single rooms. However, establishing noise levels from the beginning at a DIN level of about 35 phon means that peaks of work noise in the open-plan office become too distinct and people feel more disturbed.

The use of the same space as an open-plan office or sub-divided into single rooms also has repercussions on the electrical installation.

1.5 Electrical installation

The open-plan office has a network of electrical connections under the floor. These provide all workplaces with lighting and power supplies.

119

There is a generous provision of sockets, so that if there is any shifting of workplaces, cables do not have to be taken up with consequent disturbance of work. This expensive electrical installation is completely superfluous after sub-division into single rooms and remains unutilized.

Lighting in the open-plan office is designed at 800–1,000 lx. On later conversion into corridors and record offices some light tubes may be removed. It is doubtful, however, whether on reducing the light intensity in the single rooms, where glare may be produced by the partitions, there will be optimal lighting of the now fixed workplaces. In any case the sub-divided space will be burdened with unprofitable installation costs. In the open-plan office the lighting is switched on and off in sections. If the space is sub-divided into single rooms, conversion to individual control is possible only at great expense, as additional circuits are necessary.

1.6 Room fittings

There are some problems of fitting out, which can be solved differently in open-plan or conventional offices, but for which there is also a common solution. Carpeted floors, for example, are indispensable in the open-plan office and optional in single rooms, but too expensive in record rooms which were formerly open-plan offices.

The extent of capital outlay occasioned merely in order that the open-plan office can one day be sub-divided, and the extent of original capital outlay which becomes superfluous, once the open-plan office is conventionally sub-divided again, render it advisable to plan an open-plan or a conventional office solely as such in all respects, particularly as a compromise is not beneficial to either type. Only if a decision is made irrevocably in favour of either open-plan or cellular construction, can either of the two forms of office be built on economically sound foundations.

Paper 2

The air-conditioning plant in an open-plan office

by Hubert Brendel

The following points are of great importance in evaluating an open-plan office air-conditioning plant:

1 Optimum comfort for the occupants.
2 Acceptable capital expenditure.
3 Low operating costs.

2.1 Thermal control of the air in the room

The question of achieving optimum comfort in the premises is far and away the most important consideration to be evaluated.

As comfort depends principally on a regular heat exchange between the body and the atmosphere, room temperature, room humidity, surface temperature of the surroundings and air velocity are all of importance.

Since the air velocity in the occupied area of a room depends almost exclusively on the quantity admitted and on the guiding and distribution of the air flow, the maintenance of a predetermined room temperature is predominantly the result of satisfactory functioning of the regulating devices.

Every open-plan office contains sections with differing air-conditioning requirements, and, therefore, methods of air supply hitherto successfully used in conference halls, for example, cannot be uniformly instituted throughout the office, as has often been attempted in many completed building projects.

The window zones of an open-plan office are influenced by the most extreme outside conditions of heat and cold, whilst the inner zone has only to be cooled year in, year out, because of the constant heat from light fittings. If one imagines a dividing line through the premises at a height to depth ratio of 1:6 to 1:20, it immediately becomes clear that the air circulation in the outer and inner zones must be different; namely in the outer zone it is cylindrical, air being blown from the

121

window sill towards the ceiling, and in the inner zone it is blown from the ceiling vertically downwards into the room and is sucked away likewise *via* the ceiling.

If in addition the stream of air is conducted over the light tubes, a considerable part of the lamp heat can be directly removed, the light yield being increased by 10–13 per cent as a result of this intensive cooling.

This method allows a considerable reduction in the quantities is of air supplied and thus indirectly reduces the risk of draughts.

Even in the outer zone thermal influences must be reduced to a minimum by sensible design of glazing, blinds and sills, because only thus is it possible to manage with small quantities of circulated air and so avoid draughts.

Particular importance must also be paid to achieving a good heat balance of the occupants, especially to reducing radiation of body heat through the windows in winter by curtains, and providing the panes with an evaporated gold film and the like.

2.2 Temperature and relative humidity

Through an appropriate combination of regulating devices, temperatures do not fluctuate perceptibly from a predetermined level. The temperature adjustment is synchronized in all the zones of an open-plan office, and allows differing sectional operation according to conditions, obtaining an extraordinarily uniform temperature distribution over the whole open-plan area.

Naturally the room temperature and the room humidity must be automatically adapted to outside atmospheric conditions. Room values found to be particularly comfortable are about 22°C, 40–50 per cent relative humidity in winter and, according to outside temperature, 22 to 26°C and about 50–55 per cent relative humidity in summer.

Such values are subject to frequent criticism, but it is quite definite from various investigations that they constitute an optimum.

The minimum humidity to be maintained in the open-plan office is determined chiefly by the electrostatic charge (ion count).

2.3 Cost and productivity of an air-conditioning plant

Under present conditions the cost of a full air-conditioning plant amounts to 13–18 per cent of the total building costs but this is frequently felt to be too high and attempts are being made to cut down this expenditure drastically.

It is not always fully appreciated that this almost certainly involves a considerable increase in operating costs (power costs, operation, etc.) and loss of comfort.

Investigations in the USA have shown that well functioning air-conditioning plants produce a rise in the output of the occupants of the room of between 5·5 and 13 per cent. Moreover, it is quite common for a defective air-conditioning plant to give rise to continual and justified complaints, and this certainly does not increase output. Related to salaries and salary-associated expenses in the open-plan office, the difference in outlay between a good and a bad plant is negligible.

Naturally it is important to restrict to a minimum extra expenditure which is purely structural (room for ducts, machine rooms, etc), by exhausting all technical possibilities.

2.4 Planning of operating costs

Many open-plan blocks have been erected without even approximate estimates of the operating costs being submitted during the planning stage. This is to be attributed to the fact that many plants are built without any consideration of economical design and are operated without any regard to physical conditions.

It is therefore absolutely necessary from the outset to call in a qualified air-conditioning consultant who is an expert on such matters. If one neglects to do this, power costs may sometimes be as much as 30 to 50 per cent above what could have been achieved with positive planning.

It is naturally very difficult to determine all influences, particularly those of the weather, so that absolute consumption values can be calculated. It is necessary amongst other things to process hour-long measurements of the outside temperature, the relative humidity of the air, sun radiation, etc. taken at the place where the plant is situated over a fairly long period, e.g. 10 years, i.e. to process about 200,000 values, in order to obtain representative bases for calculation.

Also of decisive influence on the extent of the operating costs is the thermal design of the building, i.e. of the façade, glazing, walls and ceilings, the choice of blinds, the intensity of lighting provided, etc.

Current and heat consumption of the various plants must be calculated both for the operating and the idle state, and attending, maintenance and repair costs must be compiled from experimental values.

These points must be promptly and fully dealt with, if later disappointments are to be avoided.

In these considerations one must also bear in mind that conditions are different in every building and general guide-lines must be used only with the greatest caution. Only a thorough working out of each individual case will prevent trouble.

With sensible use of all the technical possibilities available today it is possible to build satisfactory and economic air-conditioning plants, provided that everyone participating in the planning and building is prepared for understanding and frank team work.

Report of the Deutsche Institut für Betriebswirtschaft (DIB)* Conference
held to pool experiences of open-plan offices, 28 October 1966

Platform: Herr Büttner (Mannheim)
Herr Jacobi (Köln-Niehl)
Herr Jeuthe (Ludwigshafen)
Dr Rodius (Nordhorn)
Herr Scholtz (Architect, Ludwigshafen)
Herr Weber (Director, Ludwigsburg)
Chairman: Herr Schuldes (Gütersloh)

3.1 Results of voting

Before the discussion the following was established by means of a vote-meter:

Who has an open-plan office?	26 per cent
Who works in an open-plan office himself?	10 per cent
Who is planning erection of an open-plan office?	54 per cent
How many of these are already at the planning stage?	46 per cent
Who has already been in an open-plan office (e.g. visits, inspections, etc.)?	76 per cent
Who has once worked in an open-plan office and got away from it?	5 per cent
Who considers the open-plan office: rather a problem of organization?	20 per cent
rather a problem of personnel management?	80 per cent
Who is against the open-plan office?	20 per cent
Who is for the open-plan office?	70 per cent
Who would prefer to await further developments?	10 per cent

* German Institute for Industrial Economy.

125

Although the voting confirmed the speakers' opinions that the open-plan office is in the first place a problem of personnel management, it was mainly the technical/organizational questions that were discussed in detail.

3.2 Questionnaire or interview?

The participants had received the results of the DIB questionnaire survey as a basis on which to work. The object of this survey, which the DIB (Frankfurt am Main) carried out in conjunction with business consultant, Axel Boje (Düsseldorf), was to gain some idea of what the workers themselves in the open-plan offices think of them.

Seven firms had agreed to this test. Open-plan offices of varying sizes had been tested: 36 work in the smallest, 350 in the largest.

There were various opinions as to the expediency of questionnaires in checking on the success of organizational measures. In the DIB's opinion an important condition of questioning workers is objectivity and anonymity. The workers cannot give an objective opinion if they have the feeling that their superiors or those responsible for the introduction of the open-plan office know what they are saying. This possibility was excluded by having the questionnaires forwarded to the DIB in a sealed envelope.

One group of participants was of the opinion that anonymity brings its own risks: their experience shows that the workers will first of all talk about the questions and opinions will then be formed by the loudest opponents or the head of the group. Although one could not question every worker individually because of the time involved, it is nevertheless more expedient to question certain selected persons in direct interview.

For example one could have one speaker chosen from each working group, who should be asked to collaborate in solving open-plan problems.

Another criticism was that questionnaires often contain leading questions, e.g.

Do you miss daylight?

Do you feel mentally secure in an open-plan office?

Even in the personal interview, leading questions cannot of course be completely excluded. The questioner may consciously or unconsciously influence the answers by the way he leads the conversation. The worker being questioned has no guarantee that what this or that worker or department head thinks of the open-plan solution will not be reported back to the management in detail.

The confidential nature of a questionnaire survey was generally confirmed.

One of the concerns tested had questionnaire surveys carried out by two institutes at different times. The entire staff of the firm was interviewed by two sociologists into the bargain. The outcome was amazing. The results of the questionnaires were largely identical and were altogether positive.

The management discovered the reason for this: on being questioned by outside sources a certain pride in the firm was exhibited because of the erection of an open-plan office, whereas the interviewers were considered as emissaries of the management, to whom a proper opinion could be given.

3.3 Architectural design

From the architect's angle the technical problems of the open-plan office have been overcome. There is scarcely any dispute over what is an optimum ground plan. Difficulties only arise when the architect is given the problem of converting a conservative office building into open-plan offices. Opinions are quite clear that an optimum solution will never be reached in this way.

As desirable as the open-plan solution may seem to the architect, because it gives him the possibility of a change from monotonous work to a dynamic style of building, single rooms are often indispensable for organizational reasons. There are then two possibilities:

1 A closed building complex with the core as a linking element between single room and open-plan office.
2 Partitioning a given open-plan area into single rooms by mobile elements which do not reach right up to the ceiling and can be taken down. They give the worker the feeling that he is sitting in a closed room, once he has shut the door behind him.

The second solution affords the opportunity of doing away with this compromise at a later date. A combination of open plan and single rooms will not be an ideal architectural solution, as the structural conditions for both types of offices are very different, particularly room depths.

It would appear advisable to enter into such compromises undogmatically and with an open mind, as the advantages which even half an open-plan office offers over the former cellular construction from the financial and organizational points of view are quite considerable.

3.4 Air-conditioning plants

The air-conditioning of open-plan offices is today no longer a technical problem to the air-conditioning engineer. Nevertheless most complaints from workers are directed against the air-conditioning plant.

Perhaps the reason for this is that in the early days of the open-plan office it was thought that plants as built in the USA could also be used for German conditions. The American, however, has a quite different attitude to air-conditioning: he feels most comfortable when he has taken his jacket off and feels the air fanning him. In German open-plan offices it is different: the most frequent complaint is 'There's a draught'.

If measurements are taken, it is often found that the air velocity fully conforms with DIN regulations. The same applies to alleged oxygen deficiency. Measurements prove that there is at least sufficient oxygen, sometimes even too much.

Another source of criticism is the room temperature. Women usually work best at a temperature of between 23 and 24°C, whilst 20 to 21°C is enough for men.

Finally relative humidity constitutes a special problem. Optimum humidity should be between 45 and 55 per cent. In this range there is no electrostatic charge. When regulating the humidity, the water consumption of flowering plants has to be taken into consideration. If the conditioning plant is switched off overnight, the air humidity is too high the next day, because the plants have meanwhile given off moisture.

The following air-conditioning requirements were drawn up:

1 When the contract for a project is being given, it is absolutely necessary to call in an air-conditioning specialist.
2 The first measurements should be taken before the office is built. Later, continual measurements should be carried out complete with furniture. A well-designed plant must moisturize and demoisturize and heat and cool correctly. It must be as draught-free as possible. The period of adjustment lasts a whole year, in order to take appropriate account of all seasons. Regulation can be made difficult if the plant is over-big for reasons of flexibility.

3 No agreement could be reached as to the most favourable moving-in date for testing the air-conditioning plant.

4 The air-conditioning plant for an open-plan office will, as a rule, require higher capital expenditure than that for a conventional office.

If an air-conditioning plant is planned and installed on these principles, particularly taking into account the question of operating costs, then with satisfactory technical functioning the only remaining grounds for complaint are subjective.

The participants agreed that one cannot satisfy everybody and that there will always be grumblers even in the open-plan office. There always comes a point when consultation and concern over the personal wishes of employees must cease and the management must provide optimum conditions for the majority of the employees, if necessary arbitrarily.

One concern which instituted its open-plan office six years ago, recorded the last of the grievances shortly after introduction, apart from a few unjustified complaints.

3.5 Lighting

An open-plan office cannot function without artificial lighting. The deeper the room is, the less use are the windows. Some firms therefore have deliberated whether to incorporate an additional skylight if possible. Ophthalmologists have established that constant artificial light is better for the eyes than daylight changing from one extreme to another. In the USA there is a large office block without windows; the occupants feel quite happy in it, according to one speaker. If, however, one decides on windows, they should be just large enough for people to be able to see whether it is raining or the sun is shining.

Continual artificial lighting has the following disadvantage: the light tubes give off heat particularly in the middle of the room; they therefore have to be constantly cooled, whilst towards the outside walls the air has to be heated in order to obtain a uniform room temperature. Continuous artificial light therefore requires a more intensive air-conditioning plant. In one firm a combined plant was built at great expense, by means of which the employees could regulate the lighting in three stages according to the brightness of the daylight. Hardly any use was made of it.

3.6 Acoustics

A considerable acoustic problem in the open-plan office is echo. It is dependent on the distance of the outside walls from one another.

The necessary minimum wall distance is about 25 m. A square ground plan is for this reason more favourable than a rectangle. These considerations led Nino (Nordhorn), for example, to have a ground plan in the form of an irregular octagon.

Reflection effects can be largely eliminated by sound-absorbing elements. Often when an open-plan office is erected, space is reserved for later extensions. This may likewise lead to impairment of acoustic conditions. An inquiry during the conference revealed no particular acoustic difficulties.

3.7 Is it worth converting a conventional office into an open-plan office?

One must check very carefully, taking into account all the aspects so far mentioned (air-conditioning, ventilation, lighting, acoustics), whether the growth rate allowed by the form of the open-plan office corresponds to present and future requirements.

Experience has shown that such a conversion in practice is not much more favourable, costs-wise, than a new building.

A new building, however, has the advantage of allowing much greater regard for specific open-plan principles. Generally speaking a conversion is not to be advised. However, such a non-ideal solution may often be the only way of getting the open-plan idea over to management and workers. Many firms have achieved extremely good results with such half-way solutions and then, building on this experience, have been able to erect other open-plan offices much more closely approaching the ideal.

3.8 Can concentrated work be performed in an open-plan office?

The importance of the single room is often defended with the argument that concentrated or creative work is impossible in an open-plan office.

If one gives way to this argument, the allocation of single rooms should be done not on a hierarchical basis, but according to the work to be performed. It is a fallacy to equate creative work with rank.

Plate 1 Open-plan office at the Volkswagen works, Wolfsburg

iew of the open-plan ... at Osram, Munich

ance to the open-plan ...e of Decker, Munich

Accountants' room with typing places of Boehringer, Mannheim

Part of the two-level open plan office of Boehringer, Mannheim

In a view of an open-plan office in the office building of Nino Nordbern

In... view of an open-plan office set up by Pohlschröder

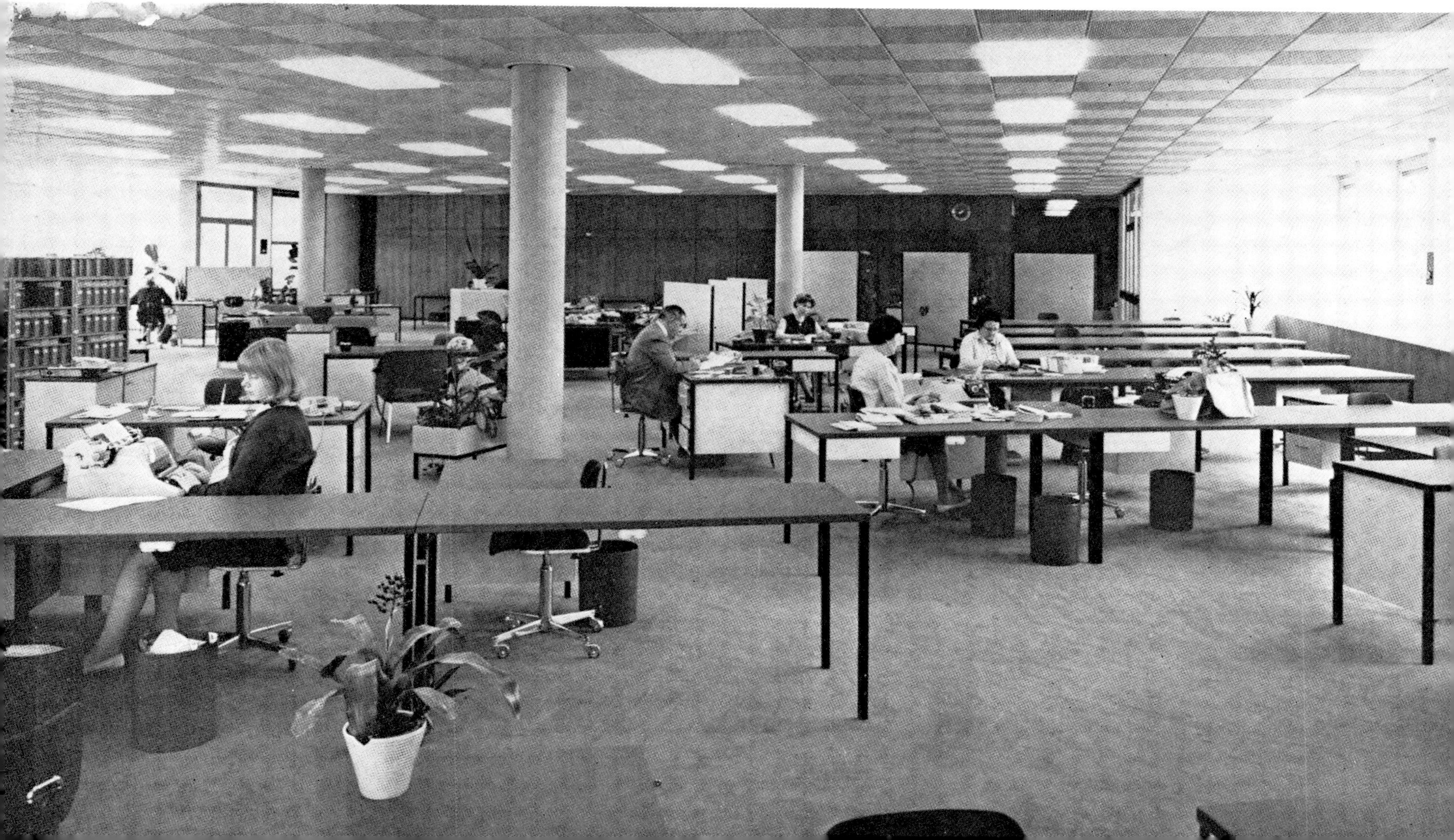

Ein moderner Großraumbüro der Albert Schäfer und Nettelmann, Bielefeld

...uilding Design, Partnership: ground floor, showing library at gallery level

Plate 16 Audiotypists on the upper floor of Boots office block, showing the courtyard in the background.

Plate 17 Carrels at Boots office.

According to one speaker, doctors have established that narrow cell-like rooms are not ideal workplaces.

Much more important than absolute quiet is the possibility of excluding all directing disturbing factors, e.g. telephones. So-called 'silent zones' have therefore been created in open-plan offices for creative work.

Examples are: in the publishing house of Buch und Ton (Gütersloh), editors, illustrators, readers and proof-readers, persons whose creative or concentrated work cannot be denied, sit in the centre of the open-plan office, in Nino, legal staff, tax specialists, organizers and other creative workers are likewise to be found in the open-plan office. Every concession can endanger the general open-plan concept.

3.9 The open-plan office as an undesirable 'platform'

A further argument of the open-plan critic is that nothing can be kept secret in the open-plan office. One can see, for example, if somebody is always talking to the personnel manager, and can draw conclusions from this.

Audibility of conversations is admittedly virtually excluded by the general noise level, but the new element is visibility. In this case interviewing cubicles are not of much help either. More frequently one hears the complaint that one cannot have suppliers or customers, who are competitors, suddenly meeting in the open-plan office.

Such meetings cannot be fully excluded even by the most skilful secretary (in the export department for example).

Such exceptions should not be over-stressed. They are no argument against the open-plan office. A story is told about two representatives from the Arab States and the Israeli Mission—great efforts were made to keep them apart by careful measures in the outer office. Owing to a mistake in the chauffeur arrangements, both gentlemen were collected from the airport in the same car.

3.10 Real disadvantages of the open-plan office

The following were given as disadvantages:

1 Extension is only possible on a large scale. A certain reserve will always be incorporated. Should this prove to be insufficient and

say 3 to 10 new workplaces be needed, enlargement is only possible within a much larger framework.

2 In cases of crisis, during notable political or local events, in exceptional situations, such as a death at work, the open-plan office is conceivably an unfavourable environment.

A general view

by Dieter Andreas

In an open-plan project comprising over 2,000 workplaces it has been established that purely technical and organizational questions make up less than 50 per cent of the total problems.

The technique of organization, the forming of types of workplace, the drawing up of principles, lighting, decoration, air-conditioning, workplace layout—these and many similar matters have been taken in hand, as it were. More difficult and time-consuming is being able to recognize and take into account the sociological and psychological aspects of the open-plan system. The open-plan office organizer's job is therefore to concern himself more with people.

The type of person suited to the open-plan office is only just coming into being. Much missionary work still needs to be done; this will not be possible without the help of industrial psychologists or sociologists. A quite positive attitude to the open-plan office can already be detected in the ordinary worker; the difficulties start in the middle ranks and increase the higher one goes in the hierarchy.

The third largest insurance company in the USA has an open-plan office containing 1,500 workers. People have become used to it and are satisfied with their new working world. The old offices were much worse.

In Germany one tends to overdo the open-plan office on economic grounds.

Furthermore, an optimum open-plan solution is endangered, if it is not preceded by, an exact planning of workplaces and department arrangement. The planning stage should be at least as long as the building period, if not longer.

The open-plan office should be planned from the inside to the outside. Before planning begins, the exact present situation should be established and analysed and from this the desirable theoretical situation should be evolved.

There is no point in tying up old faults in new parcels.

At the outset one must call in an architect who understands the concept from the beginning.

There must be no question of priorities in the team.

When planning an office building a reserve for the next 10 years must be incorporated; before the building is occupied, five years will have elapsed.

The aim of every act of office organization should be to try to gain willing workers with lasting high output.

Part D

THE OPEN-PLAN TEST

---

by Axel Boje

Chapter 1

Introduction

The attitude of organization and methods specialists, planners and architects and a limited number of organization's managements, to the open-plan office has been known for a relatively long time. The opinion of open-plan users, or executive or managing staff in open-plan offices, is, however, known only from individual statements—there has been no statistical survey of a representative minority or majority. Individual pronouncements such as these, whether they be positive or negative, do not give a realistic picture of the effect of open-plan offices on the people working in them. Although there is nothing new about the open-plan office and the modern type cannot be considered to be still in its infancy, discussions on this topic have not lessened in either frequency or intensity. Since the popular press has had occasion to take up the theme, publishing the statements of a few open-plan office users in papers with circulations of millions, the danger of one-sided emphasis being given to subjective statements of either a positive or negative nature, has been increased.

This has led to a need for objective information on the effect of the open-plan office on workers. There are about 84,000 people working in more than 2,100 open-plan offices of about 1,200 concerns in the Federal Republic of Germany. Their verdict on their working surroundings therefore merits some attention. With a still larger number of undertakings considering the change to modern open-plan offices in the next few years or decades, the development of this organizational, technical and architectural phenomenon in all its aspects—economic, psychological and sociological—is of extraordinary interest to all those who will have to make the planning decisions and for forming the opinions of the people who will be working in these open-plan offices of the future.

Out of these considerations arose the idea of a test survey on the effect of open-plan offices on office workers. The Deutsche

Institut für Betriebswirtschaft (German Institute for Industrial Economy) (Frankfurt am Main) took up the author's suggestion of this survey and undertook to administer it.

Chapter 2

The test survey

The survey was carried out in Spring 1966.

2.1 Selection of undertakings

Of the 1,200 concerns with open-plan offices known to the author, the initiators of the survey expected to receive consent to the survey from about 100 undertakings. Of these 100, they selected 40 who were known in the organizational world as having an open-plan solution good enough to serve as an example.

Forty undertakings with open-plan offices were written to by DIB as follows:

DEUTSCHES INSTITUT FÜR
BETRIEBSWIRTSCHAFT E.V.
27 January 1966

Inquiry amongst the workers in your open-plan offices

Dear Sirs,
Open-plan offices are much discussed, mostly by organization and methods experts, architects or manufacturers of office furniture. It is perhaps only the employees who work in open-plan offices that have not had sufficient opportunity to report on their experiences and impressions. However, to obtain objective information from them would be particularly instructive and valuable for firms who

1 Are discussing the question of whether they should provide open-plan offices in an administrative conversion or new building, and in what form.
2 Have already instituted an open-plan office but would like to know more exactly how the effects of this compare with other firms having open-plan offices, what the employees in the open-plan office really think, and where there is still room for improvement.

Please therefore give your workers an opportunity of expressing their opinions and reporting on their experiences, perhaps for the first time, by completing the questionnaire, a sample of which is enclosed.

We are thinking of carrying out the inquiry as follows:

1 You may tell us by telephone or letter whether you agree to the survey and how many questionnaires you require.

2 Your organization division distributes the questionnaires amongst your employees, collects the completed questionnaires and returns them all together to our Institute.

3 The evaluation will be carried out at our Institute—possibly by data-processing in a computer centre—under the technical supervision of Axel Boje Dipl.Kfm, Business Consultant, Düsseldorf.

4 You will receive from us a general evaluation as well as a comparison of the results of the individual firms, which will be denoted by code numbers. You will be informed of your own code number.

5 The evaluation of the results is to be the subject of a talk at a conference to be held here on 16 May 1966.

Please let us know soon whether you will take part in this survey. We would like to have the evaluation completed by the end of April.

Signed, etc.

Ten undertakings answered in writing and seven gave their consent and took part in the survey.

2.2 Refusals

The three concerns who had refused and the thirty who had not replied were then contacted by telephone and either would not give their reasons or gave one or more of the following:

1 Internal reasons.

2 We do not have a 'real' open-plan office.

3 We do not have a 'so-called' open-plan office.

4 We do not have open-plan offices, only 'functional offices'.

5 Answers to the questionnaire would be 'agreed' and would not be 'uninfluenced'.

6 We have had open-plan offices in use for X years with good results and would therefore rather avoid a questionnaire.

7 This complex theme cannot be rationally dealt with by a simple questionnaire. Interviewing would probably be more suitable.

8 Our workers have got used to the open-plan office (in five years); we should like to avoid renewed discussion and unsettling the firm.

9 Our open-plan solution constitutes the optimum that could be achieved. There is no need for renewed discussion without good reason.

10 We do not expect to get any additional information from your inquiry.

11 We do not have an open-plan office and shall not be having one.

Many of the undertakings who had refused declared an express interest in the result of the survey in other concerns ('We are very interested in this subject for our future new administrative buildings'; 'Please inform us very promptly of the results of the survey'; 'You will appreciate that we also attach great importance to knowing the exact opinion of our workers on this subject').

Similar considerations may have motivated the 75 per cent of concerns written to, who likewise declined to take part in the survey but without making their reasons public. The arguments given are an impressive testimony to the internal difficulties created within a firm by sociological investigations in general and by the open-plan theme in particular. They also supply a valuable basis for criticism of the method of questioning used.

Only a very superficial interpretation of the number (75 per cent) and manner of the refusals would allow the conclusion that 75 per cent of the open-plan offices considered by experts to have succeeded had in fact failed. Avoidance of questionnaires must not be equated with consciousness of a negative form of organization. Merely touching upon a delicate subject can provoke amongst office workers a change from a positive or indifferent attitude to a negative one.

2.3 Those taking part

All the more creditable is the consent of the seven undertakings who did take part in the survey. Only one of them had already planned in any case to carry out such a survey in their own firm. The other undertakings decided to take part only after very careful deliberation and one concern gave its consent only with considerable misgivings.

In the following description of the concerns taking part, the author has had to omit any details which could allow the firm to be identified, e.g. moving-in date, because of the pledge of anonymity. The following description of the participants from the point of view of organizational and room design is permissible:

Concern No.	Features
I	Textile floor covering, asymmetrical workplace arrangement, office landscape, good design.
II	Textile floor covering, mixed asymmetrical and geometric workplace arrangement, intensive inter-communication with team work, bold room design, very good spatial solution.
III	Textile floor covering, intimate atmosphere, harmonious work atmosphere (personnel division), generous and free workplace arrangement, very good spatial solution.
IV	Textile floor covering, free workplace arrangement, tense work atmosphere, good spatial solution.
V	Hard flooring, workplace arrangement in schoolroom layout, room fittings and design capable of improvement.
VI	Textile floor covering, geometrical workplace arrangement, good spatial solution.
VII	Textile floor covering, free, asymmetrical workplace arrangement, good room design.

At the time of the survey concerns I–VI had occupied open-plan offices for $1\frac{1}{2}$ to 5 years, concern VII 6–8 months.

We take this opportunity of once again thanking all the seven concerns taking part for their understanding and active assistance.

Chapter 3

The method

The initiators of this survey chose a method of questioning which seemed to ensure maximum probability of complete and accurate information on the facts being investigated, with least possible expense. The financing of the survey was done solely from the funds of the two initiating bodies with no state or other support.

3.1 Execution

The survey was executed as follows:

Idea:	Axel Boje
Basic form of questionnaire:	Axel Boje
Revision of questionnaire:	DIB
Dispatch of questionnaires:	DIB
Distribution of questionnaires:	Seven undertakings taking part
Completion and sealing of questionnaires:	Office workers in the open-plan offices of the seven undertakings taking part
Collection of questionnaires and return to DIB:	Seven undertakings taking part
Statistical collation per undertaking:	DIB
Statistical collation of all firms:	Axel Boje
Public commentary at DIB Conference:	Axel Boje
Written commentary:	Axel Boje

The results of the inquiry were published at two DIB Conferences in 1966 and 1967 and discussed with those present—mainly O & M specialists, space-planners and architects.

The DIB sent the necessary number of questionnaires, each with a seal, to the firms who had replied to the first letter, declaring their willingness to participate in the survey. The personnel management division, O & M division, departmental management or other suitable headquarters staff undertook distribution of the questionnaires to the occupants of the open-plan offices. This was sometimes done by an internal memorandum, giving some guidance as to the survey procedure and completion of the questionnaire. The employees filled in the questionnaires anonymously, sealed them and handed them to the internal collection point either singly or in batches. The firms then promptly sent the collected questionnaires to Frankfurt. The DIB received only sealed questionnaires and then began on the job of opening them and evaluating them per firm. Four weeks had been allowed for the questionnaires to remain in the firms. The actual time they remained was between 3 and 8 weeks.

Because of leave, sickness and other causes of absence, not all the open-plan occupants of the firms taking part were covered. The completion of the questionnaires by the occupants was voluntary. Of 1,580 workers in the open-plan offices 1,220 supplied completed questionnaires.

3.2 The questionnaire

Before the start of the inquiry two methods of questioning were discussed:

1 Interview.
2 Questionnaire.

The initiators of the survey decided in favour of the questionnaire, for the following reasons:

1 By the manner and phrasing of his questioning the interviewer can exert a certain influence on the answers. The initiators of the survey can only control the subjective behaviour of the interviewer to a restricted extent.

2 Because of the personal confrontation between interviewer and interviewee, the anonymity of the latter is lost. Apart from 'word of honour', the interviewee has no absolute guarantee that his answers will remain anonymous and that no personal disadvantage will ensue from honest replies. The risk of manipulated answers is therefore increased.

3 Personal interviewing of 1,220 office workers by psychologists, sociologists or other professional interviewers would incur far higher costs than a questionnaire survey.

144

4 Even with personal interviews a questionnaire would have to be evolved as a guide for the interviewer.

There are also reasons against the use of the questionnaire as a means of inquiry, but these are either of less importance or can easily be invalidated:

1 The questionnaire can be wrongly completed through error or misunderstanding. By set answers and colloquial wording this risk can be practically eliminated.

2 Individual employees may escape completing the questionnaire. This is in the nature of a voluntary survey. Employees can also refuse personal interview. Those on annual or sick leave and other absentees may not be covered by an interviewer either.

3 Those being questioned may confer with one another about their answers. This danger is not very great because they want to remain anonymous and often do not tell their colleagues their real opinion. Moreover, agreed answers may be quite accurate answers. With voluntary agreement one may assume an agreed answer that corresponds to the facts. Daily work in the open-plan office tends to form opinions, so that a certain amount of unanimity is usually present even before such a survey is carried out.

4 Set answers on the questionnaire influence the person's reply. All programmed answers on the questionnaire include both positive and negative attitudes. We do not see why the pre-printed negative answers should exert a greater influence on the questionee than the pre-printed positive answers.

The decision to use the questionnaire was taken on all these grounds*. On 17 January 1966 the DIB sent 40 accompanying letters and 40 questionnaires. When the 7 firms taking part had declared their agreement, the requisite number of questionnaires was sent to them.

* The only external opinion poll on the effect of the open-plan office on workers known hitherto [45] is restricted to a single firm, which has also taken part in the present survey, and used the personal interview.

145

DEUTSCHES INSTITUT FÜR BETRIEBSWIRTSCHAFT—DIB— FRANKFURT AM MAIN
P.O. Box 3029 Börsenstrasse 8-10   Tel. 0611/282951

OPEN-PLAN OFFICE TEST
Inquiry into the actual effects of open-plan offices

Dear Sir or Madam,

Please help us in this inquiry. We want to find out impartially how successful the open-plan office has been and why, and also whether and how it could be improved.

You are a worker in an undertaking which has been one of the first to put this new form of organization and building into practice. Your impressions are therefore particularly important and valuable. Please tell us frankly and honestly your personal opinion and experience of work in the open-plan office.

Please cross the applicable circle O and note your brief opinion on the dotted lines.

Your replies will be treated anonymously and confidentially. You may therefore fold your questionnaire inwards along the lines marked and close it with a DIB seal before handing the completed form to your organization and methods department for mass return to our Institute.

I GENERAL PARTICULARS
10 Name of firm ....
11 Department ....
12 Age ....
13 Number of workers in office ....

14 Employed on
O Sales side   O Technical Side
Detailed occupation:
O Head of Section   O Head of Department   O Head of Group
O Assistant   O Secretary   O Shorthand-Typist (Typist/Clerk)
O General Office duties, e.g. Messenger, Records

15 Is there a telephone at your workplace?

16 Do you operate
O Yes   O No
O An office machine   O Typewriter
O Calculating machine (Adding/multiplying machine)
O Book-keeping machine (invoicing   O Punched card machines
machine)

17 Before your move to the open-plan office did you have:
O Single room   O 2–4 room   O 4–10 room   O ....

2 HOW DO YOU FIND THE FITTINGS IN YOUR OPEN-PLAN OFFICE?
20 Ceilings and walls
Do you consider the sound-absorbing measures
O adequate   O inadequate   O over-done
Are the light conditions in your opinion
O adequate   O inadequate

146

21 Flooring
(a) Is it:
O carpet   O thermoplastic   O wood   O stone
O yellow   O green   O blue   O red
O black   O beige   O grey
(b) Your preference:
O   carpet   O thermoplastic   O wood   O stone
(c) What shade would you prefer in a carpet
O yellow   O green   O blue   O red   O black
O ....

22 Screens:
O too many   O too few   O are missing altogether

23 How do you find the climate in the office?
A. Summer
O all right   O too cool   O too warm
O too humid   O too dry   O draughts
B. Winter
O all right   O too cool   O too warm
O too humid   O too dry   O draughts

24 Noises in the office
Do you find the general noise of the open-plan office:
O   normal and therefore not particularly noticeable
O   disturbingly loud
O   disturbingly quiet
Do the disturbances in your open-plan office today, compared with your former work-room, seem
O greater   O less   O unchanged
In detail:
from visitors
O greater   O less   O unchanged
from telephone
O greater   O less   O unchanged
from passers by
O greater   O less   O unchanged
from conversation
O greater   O less   O unchanged
from office machines
O greater   O less   O unchanged

25 Office furniture
You have furniture of: O wood   O steel
You would prefer furniture of: O wood   O steel

26 Plants
From your impression are there
O too many   O too few   O just enough to make the office pleasant?

27 Arrangement of workplaces
Are your workplaces
O in a schoolroom layout?
O freely distributed in groups?
Do you consider workplaces should be
O in a schoolroom layout
O freely distributed in groups

28 Differentiation of superiors in the open-plan office
Do your superiors also sit in the open-plan office?
O Yes   O No
If yes

L

147

(a) O   exactly as everyone else
(b) O   as (a) but at a larger desk and in a more comfortable chair
(c) O   as (a) but behind additional screens, plants, etc.
(d) O   in a glass cubicle
(e) O   in a separate single room
What do you consider right?
O (a)   O (b)   O (c)   O (d)   O (e)

29 **Can you arrange mascots, souvenirs, flowers, pictures, etc. in your workplaces?**   O Yes   O No
Would you like to?   O Yes   O No

3 OUTPUT IN THE OPEN-PLAN OFFICE

30 **Do you work in the open-plan office more energetically and keenly than before?**
O more   O less   O unchanged

31 **Has your calculable output increased?**
O Yes   O No   (if yes, by approximately ....%)

32 **Do you make more mistakes than before?**
O Yes   O No

33 **Do you feel more tired and irritable than in your former office?**
O Yes   O No

34 **How many workplaces can you overlook from a sitting position?**
....
Would you like to overlook
O more   O less
than at present?

35 **Have you acquired through the open-plan office a greater understanding of the functions of other departments?**
O Yes   O No
Has this interested you?   O Yes   O No

36 **Has the introduction of the open-plan office saved you journeys through the building?**
O Yes   O No   (if yes, approximately ....%)

37 **As a superior has your professional contact with your workers in the open-plan office**
O improved   O not altered   O deteriorated

38 **Has your professional contact with your superiors**
O improved   O not altered   O deteriorated

39 **Since the introduction of the open-plan office has punctuality**
O increased   O decreased   O remained the same

4 PSYCHOLOGICAL EFFECTS

40 **Do you find your open-plan office**
O pleasant   O too comfortable   O too bare

41 **In the open-plan office do you feel yourself**
O unobserved   O observed
by your colleagues
O or don't you pay attention to this while working?

42 **In the open-plan office do you feel yourself**
O unobserved   O observed
by your superiors and subordinates
O or don't you pay attention to this while working?

43 **Compared with your previous office, in the open-plan office do you feel yourself mentally**
O more secure   O more lonely   O indifferent

44 **Compared with before do you feel more strongly in the open-plan office that you are**
O an individual   O a member of a group   O one of a mass

5 **GENERAL VERDICT**

50 **On the whole do you consider the open-plan office a**
O better   O worse
solution in comparison with your former office?

51 **Do you like your own workplace in the open-plan office**
O less   O more
than in your former office?
Why ....

52 **Mainly for what reasons do you think your firm's management decided on the open-plan office?**
O saving in building costs
O output improvement in work flow
O flexibility on growing or shrinking of various departments, with the result that the office building does not get out of date so quickly
O better supervision of workers
O publicity for the firm
O hobby of management
O open-plan offices are modern
O other reasons ....

53 **Do you consider this/these reason(s) valid in our present economy?**
O Yes   O No

54 **Do you enjoy it when your open-plan office is an object of interest to press, television and visitors, and also to your own relatives and friends?**
O Yes   O No

6 **CONSEQUENCES**

60 **Do you remain with your firm**
O in spite of the open-plan office
O because of the open-plan office
O for reasons which have nothing to do with the open-plan office?

61 **If you were a member of the management, what would you have done differently?** ....
....

3.3 Questionnaire content

A few remarks are necessary concerning the methodical structure of the questionnaire. Whilst some of the set answers are formulated as alternatives, in various questions a plural answer is also possible, e.g. Q52. In the second case answers are more than 100 per cent. This cannot be considered a disadvantage, however, if several influencing factors act conjointly. In some cases a double question is contained in

149

one nominal question, e.g. Q23—Climate in summer—: too humid—too dry—draughts. Separation into independent single questions would doubtless be better, e.g. too humid—too dry—all right—draughts—no draughts. This analysis would have extended the questionnaire however. Experience shows that willingness to complete questionnaires decreases with the extent of the questions. Often an intentionally missing alternative has been correctly inserted by the questionee, e.g.:

1 Q34 desired overlooking of workplaces.
   In the questionnaire: more—less.
   Added by the questionee: satisfied.
2 Q51 verdict on own workplace.
   In the questionnaire: less good—better.
   Added by the questionee: just as good.

These missing alternative answers are methodically intended to provoke a creative reply and at the same time test how well developed the personal opinion is. The frequency of these additions is to be considered as a positive sign of the credibility of the answers.

Now a few remarks on the material content of the questionnaire. In the set answers to certain questions the questionnaire naturally also includes negative room features or details, e.g. Q21—Flooring of thermoplastic, wood, etc. A restriction to positive forms would be considered non-objective, and the intention is to bring out the effects of positive or negative fittings. Naturally one cannot compare the statements from different firms without considering such differences in fittings. Averaging from positively and negatively fitted open-plan offices is of course not possible.

The alternative answers in the questionnaire were in some cases criticized at the DIB Conference in 1966 as being unscientific or not strictly serious, e.g. Q52—Hobby of management. To the same end are aimed objections that the set answer could induce unqualified answers given for effect, e.g. Q43—Do you feel mentally more isolated in the open-plan office than in your former office? or Q44—Do you feel more strongly in the open-plan office that you are one of a mass?

These objections are justified as far as the level of expression is concerned. However, a higher scientific level of expression would certainly cause misunderstanding. A more extended wording which would avoid such colloquialisms, would have considerably complicated the questionnaire. Popular wording makes it simpler to complete the form more than it impairs material accuracy.

The questions asking for the questionee's wishes, e.g. Q21, Q25, Q27, Q29, naturally do not contain any kind of promise that these wishes will be fulfilled. Neither the initiators of the survey nor the firms taking part had given their open-plan occupants such an undertaking. It is naturally altogether doubtful whether the office employees in an open-plan office see all the influencing factors clearly and whether their wishes would correspond to an expertly based opinion. Thus, for example, in the question on desired flooring colour (Q21), the open-plan office users can only be expected to give a subjective and emotional opinion, whilst space planners and architects must select the colour for harmony of furniture and floor, for harmony with lighting, susceptibility to dirt and psychological and emotional effects. Many authorities are of the opinion that the employees should choose the colours of their room themselves; however, this is not the opinion of the vast majority of space planners or of the author. It can never do any harm to ask employees about colours. If the answers show a wide diversity, they can be ignored. If the majority are in agreement, they merit some notice.

3.4 Evaluation

In the table of results the firms taking part are arranged according to evaluation in decreasing order of degree of satisfaction of the open-plan office users. Measured by the general verdict on the open-plan solution (Q50), the undertaking with 74 per cent approval of the open-plan office is in first place, and that with 7 per cent last (VI). This order corresponds to the order in Section 2.3. Only undertaking VII had to be omitted from this order and put at the end, because of the special circumstances arising from three different open-plan offices with differing room fittings and very diverse general verdicts. Moreover the third open-plan office of undertaking VII (180 workers) occupies a special position compared with all other firms questioned, because this office is occupied by 90 per cent technical staff, whilst the proportion of technicians in the open-plan office in the other undertakings questioned is always less than 10 per cent.

The total of answers to one question is in some cases more than 100 per cent, e.g. Q16 and Q52. In such cases more than one alternative applies, e.g. Q16—operation of two or more machines; Q52—two or more reasons considered. These multiple answers correspond to the facts. The results of answers are occasionally below 100 per cent, e.g. Q14, Q16 and others, because many open-plan occupants made

151

remarks which did not fit into the plan of the questionnaire, e.g. subjective and individual additions which could not figure in the overall evaluation because of their exceptional nature.

In some cases whole sets of questions were not answered by any of the occupants of the open-plan office (undertaking VII). In Q23B no answer could be given because there was as yet no experience (winter). (In this concern the inquiry took place at a later date than in concerns I–VI, in autumn 1966.) No reply to other sets of questions by this firm (e.g. Q25, Q28, Q29, Q35 and others) was due to internal instructions from the management of this firm that these questions were not to be answered.

The questionnaires were evaluated according to the form and order of the individual positions. It would doubtless have been possible to evaluate the individual answers to a greater extent according to various other criteria and statistical categories, e.g. differentiating answers to Q20, Q21, Q22, Q23 and Q24 according to sex. Limited financial means did not allow such a differentiation, however. Only the most important questions, Q50 and Q51—General verdict on the open-plan office and own workplace—were differentiated according to age group.

Experience gained from carrying out the survey, in the evaluation of the completed questionnaires received and during the discussion of results at the two DIB conferences, renders a revised wording of the questionnaire advisable for later similar general surveys or for interested concerns, who would like to carry out such an inquiry within their own firm.

I GENERAL PARTICULARS

10   Name of firm
11   Department
12   Age   O   under 30   O   30–45   O   over 45
13   Sex   O   male   O   female
14   Number of workers in office
15   **Employed on**   O   Sales side   O   Technical side
     Detailed occupation:
     O   Head of Section   O   Head of Department
     O   Head of Group   O   Assistant   O   Secretary
     O   Shorthand/Typist (Typist/Clerk)
     O   General Office duties, e.g. Messenger, Records
16   **How long have you been in this open-plan office?**
     O   up to 1 year   O   more than 1 year

---

17 Is there a telephone at your workplace?
O Yes   O No

18 Do you operate
O No office machine   O Typewriter
O Calculating machine (adding multiplying machine)
O Book-keeping machines (invoicing machine)
O Punched card machines

19 Before your move to the open-plan office did you have:
O Single room   O 2–4 room   O 4–10 room
O room with more than 10 persons

2 HOW DO YOU FIND THE FITTINGS IN YOUR OPEN-PLAN OFFICE?

20 Ceilings and walls
Do you consider the sound-absorbing measures
O adequate   O inadequate   O over-done
Are the light conditions in your opinion
O adequate   O inadequate

21 Flooring
(a) Is it:
O carpet   O thermoplastic   O wood   O stone
O yellow   O green   O blue   O red
O black   O beige   O grey
(b) Your preference:
O carpet   O thermoplastic   O wood
(c) What shade would you prefer in a carpet
O yellow   O green   O blue   O red   O black
O beige   O grey

22 Screens
O too many   O too few   O are missing altogether

23 Air-conditioning plant
(a) Is there one?   O Yes   O No
(b) How do you find the climate in the office?
A. Summer
O all right   O too cool   O too warm
O all right   O too humid   O too dry
O draughts   O no draughts
B. Winter
O all right   O too cool   O too warm
O too humid   O too dry   O draughts

24 Noises in the office
Do you find the general noise of the open-plan office
O normal and therefore not particularly noticeable
O disturbingly loud
O disturbingly quiet
Do the disturbances in your open-plan office today, compared with your former work-room, seem
O greater   O less   O unchanged
In detail
from visitors
O greater   O less   O unchanged
from telephone
O greater   O less   O unchanged
from passers by
O greater   O less   O unchanged

from conversation
O greater   O less   O unchanged
from office machines
O greater   O less   O unchanged

25 Office furniture
You have furniture of: O wood   O steel
   (material of top and pedestals)
O with solid sides   O without solid sides
You would prefer furniture of: O wood   O steel
O with solid sides (solid furniture)
O without solid sides (skeleton furniture)

26 Plants
From your impression are there
O too many   O too few   O just enough to make the office
                                              pleasant?

27 Can you arrange mascots, souvenirs, flowers, pictures, etc., in your workplaces?   O Yes   O No
Would you like to?   O Yes   O No

28 Arrangement of workplaces
Are your workplaces:
O in block arrangement
O in a schoolroom layout
O freely distributed in groups
O in a combination of arrangements
Do you consider workplaces should be
O in block arrangement
O in a schoolroom layout
O freely distributed in groups
O a combination of these arrangements

29 Differentiation of superiors in the open-plan office. Does your boss also sit in the open-plan office?
O Yes   O No
If yes
(a) O with the same workplace fittings as everyone else
(b) O at a larger desk and in a more comfortable chair
(c) O behind additional screens, plants, etc.
What do you consider right?
O in open-plan office   O in single room
Fittings O (a)   O (b)   O (c)

3 OUTPUT IN THE OPEN-PLAN OFFICE

30 Do you work in the open-plan office more energetically and keenly than before?
O more   O less   O unchanged

31 Has your calculable output increased?
O Yes (if yes, by approximately ....%)   O No

32 Do you make more mistakes than before?
O Yes   O No

33 Do you feel more tired and irritable than in your former office?
O Yes   O No

34 Has the introduction of the open-plan office saved you journeys through the building?
O Yes (if yes, approximately ....%)   O No

35 How many workplaces can you overlook from a sitting position?
....

Would you like to overlook
O more   O less
than at present?

36 Have you acquired through the open-plan office a greater understanding of the functions of other departments?
O Yes   O No
Has this interested you?   O Yes   O No

37 As a superior has your professional contact with your workers in the open-plan office
O improved   O not altered   O deteriorated

38 Has your professional contact with your superiors
O improved   O not altered   O deteriorated

39 Since the introduction of the open-plan office has punctuality
O increased   O decreased   O remained the same

4 PSYCHOLOGICAL EFFECTS

40 Do you find your open-plan office
O pleasant   O too comfortable   O too bare

41 In the open-plan office do you feel yourself
O unobserved   O observed
by your colleagues
O or don't you pay attention to this while working?

42 In the open-plan office do you feel yourself
O unobserved   O observed
by your superiors and subordinates
O or don't you pay attention to this while working?

43 Compared with your former office, in the open-plan office do you feel yourself mentally
O more secure   O more lonely   O indifferent

44 Compared with before do you feel more strongly in the open-plan office that you are
O an individual   O a member of a group   O one of a mass

5 GENERAL VERDICT

50 On the whole do you consider the open-plan office a
O better   O worse
solution in comparison with your former office?

51 Do you like your own workplace in the open-plan office
O less   O more
than in your former office?
Why?...

52 Mainly for what reasons do you think your firm's management decided on the open-plan office?
O saving in building costs
O output improvement in work flow
O flexibility for growing or shrinking of various departments, with the result that the office building does not get out of date so quickly
O better supervision of workers
O publicity for the firm
O hobby of management
O open plan offices are modern
O ....

53 Do you consider this/these reason(s) valid in our present economy?
O Yes   O No

54 Do you enjoy it when your open-plan office is an object of interest to press, television and visitors, and also to your own relatives and friends?

O Yes   O No

6 CONSEQUENCES

60 **Do you remain with your firm**
O   in spite of the open-plan office
O   because of the open-plan office
O   for reasons which have nothing to do with the open-plan office?

61 **If you were a member of the management, what would you have done differently?**
Lighting ....
Noise reduction ....
Fitting out ....
Workplace arrangement ....
Furniture ....
Other ....

Chapter 4

Results

Collation of the questionnaires sent in according to firms in decreasing order of acceptance of the open-plan office (excluding VII) supplies the results shown in Table 4.1.

Table 4.1 Test results

	Firm	I	II	III	IV	V	VI	VII a	VII b	VII c	Total
Data	*Open-plan offices*	1	4	1	2	3	1	1	1	1	*Total*
	Area, m²	2,500	1,100	380	900	1,000	420	1,800	1,600	2,000	
Total staff		300	6,000	4,000	600	400	800	11,000			13,100
Number of office workers		250	400	500	200	350	140	2,000			3,840
Workers in open-plan offices:	Total	200	350	36	170	300	40	150	140	180	1,580
	%	90	90	7	85	88	30	23			42
Questionnaires returned		136	310	32	135	266	30	101	82	118	1,220
14 Employed on:		%	%	%	%	%	%	%	%	%	
Sales side		37	45	63	32	89	100	95	100	10	
Technical side		—	9	—	—	—	—	5	—	90	
Other		63	46	37	68	11	—	—	—	—	
Head of section		4	3	—	4	—	—	—	6	—	
Head of department		7	7	6	7	—	3	8	9	3	
Head of group		9	5	3	11	8	3	14	16	15	
Assistant		65	38	40	40	65	17	60	39	64	
Secretary		3	6	—	—	—	3	8	10	4	
Shorthand typist		—	9	28	—	—	20	8	10	6	
General duties		4	10	6	39	—	—	2	10	7	
Other		9	23	24	—	27	54	—	—	—	
15 Telephone at workplace:											
Yes		52	85	64	82	66	63	98	66	93	
No		43	5	21	16	27	27	2	34	7	
Other		4	10	14	—	11	—	—	—	—	
16 Operation of:											
no office machine		43	22	3	46	44	—	61	29	76	
typewriter		13	48	64	24	23	90	19	23	11	
calculating machine		24	32	6	13	14	90	23	39	11	
book-keeping/invoicing machine		4	4	6	—	5	13	1	—	—	
punched card machine		4	—	—	5	—	—	2	18	—	
other		—	—	—	—	—	—	—	—	—	
17 Previously in:											
single room		16	10	12	10	8	13	20	17	11	
2–4-person room		30	24	43	21	18	53	44	33	21	
4–10-person room		21	27	21	11	13	13	24	25	44	
open-plan office		12	—	—	34	28	3	12	25	25	
other		21	15	24	25	32	17	—	—	—	

Table 4.1 continued

		I	II	III	IV	V	VI	VII a	b	c
2 Fittings of open-plan office										
20 Ceilings and walls										
Sound	adequate	72	64	34	57	23	27	22	27	37
absorption	inadequate	23	36	52	39	78	70	78	68	63
	overdone	—	—	14	1	1	3	—	—	—
	other	—	—	—	3	—	—	—	5	—
Light	adequate	88	74	83	91	63	77	75	90	100
	inadequate	8	15	—	8	26	23	23	10	—
	other	4	11	17	1	—	—	2	—	—
21 Flooring:										
Existing	carpet	96	79	89	99	16	100	100	100	100
	thermoplastic	2	10	6	1	25	—	—	—	—
	wood	—	—	—	—	53	—	—	—	—
	stone	—	—	—	—	—	—	—	—	—
	other	—	—	—	—	—	—	—	—	—
Preferred	carpet	96	74	73	92	26	100	96	85	97
	thermoplastic	2	3	—	1	41	—	3	10	3
	wood	—	1	—	—	13	—	—	3	—
	other	—	14	—	—	20	—	1	2	—
Desired shade	yellow	58	1	3	9	2	—	84	68	93
	green	18	8	58	37	35	20	3	9	3
	blue	13	68	21	32	8	30	5	6	2
	red	2	4	—	5	9	—	—	1	—
	black	3	1	—	1	1	10	1	7	1
	other	5	18	11	—	43	33	—	4	—
				Beige 6	Gray 4 Brown 7 Beige 2	Gray 3		Beige 2 Gray 9	Orange 5	Beige 9 Gray 5
22 Screens:										
	too many	14	14	3	9	3	—	7	2	7
	too few	45	37	43	52	14	73	58	31	52
	missing	—	3	3	10	41	27	—	—	—
	adequate	14	12	—	6	—	—	3	59	41
	other	27	35	51	24	41	—	2	8	—
23 Climate										
Summer:	all right	25	31	12	39	12	—	27	5	28
	too cool	9	12	—	—	5	—	16	—	26
	too warm	54	27	70	50	48	87	48	93	36
	other	—	—	—	—	—	—	—	—	—
	too humid	4	—	—	7	—	—	9	7	—
	too dry	32	30	—	22	22	53	44	53	22
	draughts	11	23	—	22	46	23	37	30	43
	other	—	—	—	—	—	—	—	—	—
Winter:	all right	24	25	6	35	19	7			
	too cool	18	15	9	7	11	—			
	too warm	40	21	34	10	22	37			
	other	—	—	—	—	—	—			
	too humid	—	1	—	1	—	—			
	too dry	36	35	61	32	38	70			
	draughts	33	27	40	36	43	33			
	other	—	—	—	—	—	—			
24 Noise (and disturbances)										
	not noticeable	75	54	37	59	27	10	22	27	27
	disturbingly loud	18	27	34	32	55	73	60	47	25
	disturbingly quiet	4	10	21	6	7	17	18	21	38
	other	3	10	8	4	11	—	—	5	—

Table 4.1 continued

		I	II	III	IV	V	VI	VII a	VII b	VII c
Compared with formerly:	greater	30	40	37	44	48	80	79	54	47
	less	28	18	18	7	9	3	16	20	35
	unchanged	29	21	28	33	26	7	5	26	18
	other	13	21	17	16	17	10	—	—	—
From visitors:	greater	40	33	25	33	11	33	72	44	45
	less	15	10	12	11	7	—	12	12	32
	unchanged	34	33	46	42	35	53	16	40	23
	other	10	25	17	14	47	13	—	4	—
From telephone:	greater	23	34	40	23	28	47	67	40	40
	less	21	11	9	10	7	7	18	16	35
	unchanged	44	31	34	52	30	27	15	42	25
	other	13	24	17	15	35	20	—	2	—
From passers by:	greater	37	40	31	37	33	40	84	61	67
	less	15	8	18	5	4	—	11	7	22
	unchanged	37	27	31	42	27	53	5	29	11
	other	12	25	20	16	36	7	—	3	—
From conversation:	greater	27	36	49	45	44	73	75	51	42
	less	23	12	3	4	3	—	15	10	38
	unchanged	40	25	34	36	21	23	10	37	20
	other	11	27	14	15	32	3	—	2	—
From office machines:										
	greater	28	40	46	30	17	80	80	55	52
	less	29	16	12	7	8	—	8	7	24
	unchanged	29	23	25	41	32	13	12	36	24
	other	14	22	17	22	44	7	—	2	—

25 Office furniture

Existing:

	I	II	III	IV	V	VI	VII a	VII b	VII c
of wood	76	58	80	82	83	100	—		
of steel	53	32	28	27	19	7	—		
other	—	—	—	—	—	—	—		

Preferred:

	I	II	III	IV	V	VI	VII a	VII b	VII c
of wood	56	52	55	59	41	67	47	20	31
of steel	21	21	6	29	—	7	48	62	69
other	24	—	39	—	—	—	—	18	—

26 Plants

	I	II	III	IV	V	VI	VII a	VII b	VII c
too many	4	1	—	3	2	—	1	5	—
too few	23	11	—	9	35	63	21	11	23
pleasant	74	78	89	84	51	37	78	79	77
other	—	10	—	5	12	—	—	5	—

27 Workplace arrangement

Existing:

	I	II	III	IV	V	VI	VII a	VII b	VII c
schoolroom layout	26	37	—	44	79	93	5	—	—
free groups	71	52	89	57	8	7	85	100	100
other	—	—	—	—	12	—	10	—	—

More favourable:

	I	II	III	IV	V	VI	VII a	VII b	VII c
schoolroom layout	7	7	—	7	20	10	1	—	12
free groups	79	71	73	93	49	67	81	47	73
								25 mixed	15
other	15	22	27	2	32	23	18	28	

28 Superiors in open-plan office

Existing:

	I	II	III	IV	V	VI	VII a	VII b	VII c
Yes	96	73	77	99	68	23	93	82	97
No	—	3	9	1	23	77	7	18	3

Fittings:

	I	II	III	IV	V	VI
like everyone else	54	29	9	36	41	17
larger desk and chair	12	48	64	30	15	3
additional screens and plants	52	44	49	64	6	3

Table 4.1 continued

		I	II	III	IV	V	VI	VII a	VII b	VII c
in glass cubicle		—	5	—	1	15	—			
in separate single room		—	1	3	2	11	27			
other		—	—	—	—	—	—			
Opinion:										
like others		55	36	3	24	30	7	22	39	32
larger desk, etc.		4	27	37	17	9	—	18	12	20
additional screens, etc.		38	24	21	50	5	7	39	28	42
in glass cubicle		1	3	3	5	5	—	9	2	12
in single room		4	9	25	8	24	73	21	12	7
other		—	—	—	—	—	—	6	—	—
29 Flowers, pictures, etc. in workplace										
Permissible:	yes	51	25	25	62	29	43			
	no	47	65	61	39	59	57			
	other	2	10	14	—	—	—			
Reference	yes	31	23	9	35	61	13			
	no	63	64	77	63	26	83			
	other	6	2	14	—	—	—			
3 Output in open-plan office										
30 Energy and keenness:										
	more	32	21	9	16	6	—	22	48	52
	less	3	7	3	13	31	37	77	52	—
	unchanged	60	55	73	61	50	63	1	—	48
	other	5	18	14	11	12	—	—	—	—
31 Calculable output increased										
	yes	29	15	3	13	11	7	10	16	17
	by, %	—	—	—	—	—	—	—	—	—
	no	47	55	64	66	62	83	90	84	81
	other	24	31	33	21	26	10	—	—	—
32 More mistakes	yes	4	7	9	13	27	30	35	22	19
	no	86	71	70	74	56	63	65	74	81
	other	10	21	20	13	18	7	—	2	—
33 More tired and irritable										
	yes	29	43	40	42	47	73	69	68	51
	no	66	40	43	50	33	20	29	28	49
	other	4	17	17	8	21	7	2	4	—
34 Workplaces overlooked										
Number		—	—	—	—	—	—	10–30	6–20	25–30
Preference:	more	5	8	9	4	10	—	2	6	3
	less	52	51	55	55	54	90	73	30	52
	satisfied	43	41	36	41	—	—	25	64	45
35 Understanding for other departments										
Existing	yes	85	60	37	59	21	37	15	28	40
	no	12	25	43	33	61	50	83	64	60
	other	4	15	21	8	18	13	2	8	—
Interest	yes	86	77	43	62	37	50			
	no	5	17	18	22	37	40			
	other	9	16	39	16	26	10			
36 Saving of journeys										
	yes	75	75	18	36	12	33	31	45	62
	%	—	—	—	—	—	—	10–25	10–30	30
	no	14	21	61	52	65	53	67	51	38
	other	11	4	20	12	—	13	2	4	—
37 Contact with workers										
	improved	29	15	3	19	4	3	33	44	60
	not altered	11	25	31	36	32	13	65	52	40
	deteriorated	2	1	—	1	3	—	—	—	—
	other	—	—	—	—	—	—	2	4	—

Table 4.1 continued

	I	II	III	IV	V	VI	VII a	VII b	VII c
38 Contact with superiors									
improved	39	21	6	25	12	—	24	27	35
not altered	46	56	70	65	62	80	70	66	65
deteriorated	2	1	—	2	7	3	—	7	—
other	16	23	24	8	19	17	6	—	—
39 Punctuality									
increased	18	10	—	16	7	—	6	34	18
decreased	3	7	—	4	3	3	8	4	10
unchanged	68	65	89	76	74	90	78	62	72
other	10	18	11	3	16	7	8	—	—
4 Psychological effects									
40 Room found:									
pleasant to be in	78	57	80	61	13	13	46	78	71
observed	5	3	—	3	1	—	4	4	3
pay no attention	7	21	—	32	73	70	50	13	26
other	10	20	20	4	13	17	—	5	—
41 By colleagues									
unobserved	10	7	6	4	—	—	57	56	98
observed	10	13	6	19	24	30	43	42	2
pay no attention	77	71	70	77	64	70	—	2	—
other	3	10	17	—	12	—	—	—	—
42 By superiors and subordinates									
unobserved	11	12	12	7	2	3	68	66	74
observed	30	17	—	27	24	30	28	33	26
pay no attention	59	63	77	66	62	67	4	1	—
other	—	8	11	—	12	—	—	—	—
43 Mentally									
more secure	25	23	21	14	8	7	12	15	22
more lonely	9	6	3	6	17	3	—	—	—
indifferent	42	35	25	50	49	57	83	77	79
other	24	37	51	30	26	34	5	8	—
44 Group feeling									
individual	10	8	9	8	5	—	15	12	12
member of a group	63	44	55	45	25	30	33	47	69
one of a mass	16	25	6	31	54	67	52	38	19
other	10	24	30	16	16	3	—	3	—
5 General verdict									
50 Open-plan solution									
better	74	65	61	60	16	7	28	59	64
worse	14	17	15	27	66	93	71	37	36
other	13	18	24	13	18	—	1	4	—
51 Own workplace									
less good	23	19	12	37	66	83	59	23	31
better	63	58	73	41	15	10	29	57	52
equally good	14	23	14	22	20	7	12	20	17

Table 4.1 continued

	I	II	III	IV	V	VI	VII		
							a	b	c

Positive   *Negative*

Reasons

I   Better contact; better and faster information   Too many disturbances; lack of space

II   More contact with colleagues; better work flow; good allocation of space; modern furniture; fewer journeys   Poor concentration; distraction; too loud; poor air-conditioning plant

III   Faster work flow; modern fittings; generous spatial design; good contact; improved light and air

IV   Light; clean rooms; fast and better information; better contact; better co-operation   Distraction; lack of space; no concentration; poor ventilation and bad workplace arrangement

V

VI   Bad concentration

     ⎧ Modern room fittings; new office furniture, plants   Disturbances; lack of space; air-conditioning plant; lighting

VII   ⎨ Modern room fittings; new-office furniture   Disturbances; distribution of area; air-conditioning; lighting

     ⎩ Modern room fittings; new office furniture; saving of time and journeys   Disturbances; air-conditioning plant

	I	II	III	IV	V	VI	VIIa	VIIb	VIIc
52 Reasons for management's decision									
Saving in building costs	13	20	6	19	29	20	36	16	22
Improved output	74	58	37	48	24	60	23	29	33
Flexibility	25	39	15	28	9	23	28	17	47
Supervision	21	16	15	41	39	37	25	20	22
Publicity	13	29	15	15	4	33	13	25	11
Hobby of management	3	3	6	4	5	—	31	4	16
Modernity	9	17	40	22	17	33	27	25	32
other							20	20	
							former lack of space	Instructions from the top	
53 Reasons									
valid	75	70	3	71	31	43	30	53	51
invalid	13	11	49	24	45	57	60	33	49
other	13	18	48	5	25	—	10	14	—
54 Own interest in publicity									
yes	70	66	49	70	19	13	12	49	40
no	18	19	28	22	56	77	88	39	60
other	13	16	24	9	25	—	—	12	—

6 Consequences

	I	II	III	IV	V	VI
60 Do you remain with your firm						
in spite of the open-plan office	10	10	—	14	16	3
because of the open-plan office	7	6	—	4	1	—
independently of the open-plan office	78	71	83	83	68	83
other	—	—	17	—	—	—

162

Table 4.1 continued

	Lighting	Air-conditioning Sound absorption	General arrangement of layout	Furniture Workplace arrangement
61 Desired improvements				
I	Higher ceiling; more natural light	Better air-conditioning plant; better colour combinations	Cloakroom on same floor; noisy departments should be separated	Closed desks
II	More daylight. Protection from glare	Better air-conditioning; opening windows	Quietly closing doors; isolate calculating dept; closed interviewing and conference rooms; telephone centre	Closed desks; larger desks
III		Better air-conditining plant; better sound absorption; no synthetic fibre carpet because of static electricity	Separate cloakroom with hair-dressing facilities, closed rest rooms	
IV		Better air-conditioning plant; better sound absorption; better floor; separate section for heavy smokers	Separate visitors' room; more screens and flowers; isolate noisy departments	Modern and larger desks; free group arrangement; centre aisle; desks with fronts
		Better air-conditioning; better sanitary installations	Better space allocation	
VI		Better ventilation; more sound-absorption	More screens; isolate machines	More open workplace arrangement
VII	Better light; higher ceiling	Better ventilation; remove noisy machines	Divide off interviewing and conference rooms	Freer workplace arrangement, only certain departments in open-plan office, separation of executive staff
	Better lighting; higher ceiling	Better air-conditioning; isolate sources of noise	Better decoration; toilets nearer	Generous area distribution; freer workplace arrangement; more suitable furniture
	Better lighting; higher ceiling	Better air-conditioning; more sound-absorption	Better organizational planning of functions; shorter distances	Functional workplace arrangement

M

163

Chapter 5

Commentary

The results of this inquiry only allow one to make observations about the undertakings and the open-plan office users taking part. Generalization is hardly possible when out of 1,200 undertakings in the Federal Republic only 7 were included in the survey, and of approximately 84,000 persons working in open-plan offices we have the opinions of only 1,220. However, for the concerns taking part the statements of the open-plan office users can be considered as representative. An average proportion of 42 per cent of open-plan staff, measured against the total number of employees in these 7 undertakings, constitutes a considerable proportion of the personnel, and a reply rate of about 80 per cent of open-plan office users in the survey means that a high degree of reliability can be placed on their statements.

5.1 General particulars

Sizes of the open-plan offices taking part in the survey vary from 360 to 2,500 m². The proportion of workers in open-plan offices related to the total number of office workers varies from 7 to 90 per cent, and is on an average 42 per cent. The ratio of workers completing questionnaires to the total number of open-plan office users bears no relation to the positive or negative attitude to the open-plan office and can therefore be considered as being due to chance (sickness, leave, etc.).

With regard to the size of the open-plan offices, firm III with 36 workers in the open-plan office and 61 per cent approval, shows that an open-plan office does not have to be as large as many people think. Conversely the size of an open-plan office is in itself not sufficient to ensure satisfaction of the office users. In the 1,000 m² open-plan office of firm V only 16 per cent of the occupants are satisfied.

Q14 The omission of occupation on many of the questionnaires is due to the fact that simple division into sales and technical side is no longer apt in the present-day business world. Non-sales persons are by no means technical staff and vice-versa. The proportion of heads of sections and departments to the total number of employees is normal. In firm VII the proportion of group heads seems higher than average.

Q15 In open-plan design a telephone at the workplace contributes to an increase in noise density (cf. VII, II and IV). A relatively small number of telephones (I) does not hamper a positive attitude to the open-plan office and does not once prevent approval of the system of communication (Q51).

Q16 The extent of operation of office machines is a criterion of the noise intensity in the open-plan office, but the high proportion of workplaces without any office machine in firm VII does not necessarily produce overwhelming approval of the open-plan office (cf. Q50), whilst the presence of punched card machines in the open-plan office (VIIb) still allows 59 per cent approval (Q50).

Q17 A minority of at most 34 per cent (firm IV) had personal experience of an open-plan office before moving into these new offices. The majority of those questioned had hitherto spent their working lives in single or multi-person rooms.

5.2 Fitting out

Q18 The fitting out of the open-plan office is the most important criterion of acceptance or rejection by users of the open-plan office (cf. Q50). The insufficient sound-absorption criticized in concerns V–VII would appear to be the most cogent reason for rejection of the open-plan system in these concerns. Lighting is in all cases considered to be adequate.

Q21 A single firm (V) has largely no carpeted floors, thereby increasing sound reflection and providing the basis for rejection of the open-plan office by 66 per cent of the personnel. Significantly, the staff of this concern is not aware that the reason is to be found in the lack of carpeted flooring (cf. Q21—firm V). Very striking is the large number choosing yellow for the carpet colour (firms I and VII), then follow blue (firm II: 68 per cent) and green (firm III: 58 per cent). In all three firms mentioned, the users of the open-plan office prefer the carpet colour that is actually present. This fact allows both of positive and negative interpretations.

Q22 In the negative verdict of firms VI and VII there is a lack of screens in the occupants' opinion.

Q23 Even the positive verdict firms are dissatisfied with air-conditioning plants. The majority find the atmosphere too warm. The high percentage of such complaints in VI and VII (78 per cent and 93 per cent) is a major source of dissatisfaction. Although dryness of the air or draughts are complained about by only 20–50 per cent, this percentage must still be considered too high and as another grievance. This applies both in summer and winter.

Q24 In the negative verdict of firms V, VI and VII noises and disturbances are considered particularly annoying. The majority of these open-plan office users consider this negative influence greater in the open-plan office than in their former offices. Disturbances by visitors are considered greater than in conventional offices by more than a third of the open-plan office users. For 'more disturbance from telephone' and 'unchanged' the scales are about even. Disturbance from passers-by is considered greater by the majority of open-plan office users. This agrees clearly with experiences of office designers. A new discovery, on the other hand, is the fact that disturbance from conversation is also considered greater than formerly by the majority of open-plan office users. Only concerns VI and VII consider disturbance by office machines greater, 20–40 per cent of workplaces in concern VII and about 100 per cent in concern VI being equipped with office machines.

Q25 Firms I–VI prefer wood furniture, firm VII mainly steel furniture. Similarly to carpet colour, the employees prefer what they already have.

Q26 Plant arrangements in the open-plan office are in the main considered to be pleasant.

Q27 The arrangement of workplaces in free groups or in asymmetrical form is obviously popular. A combination of schoolroom layout, block form and free grouping is also desired.

Q28 With the exception of firm VI immediate superiors are located in the open-plan office in all the concerns taking part. The majority are provided with larger desk tops, more comfortable seating arrangements, additional screens and plant troughs. It is interesting to note that the majority of employees approve and sanction these more expensive fittings for superiors. This is probably because the individual hopes to occupy such a position himself one day. Very striking is the proportion of open-plan office users, in some cases 20 per cent (firms III, V, VII) and in one case as much as 73 per cent (firm VI) who would like the boss to have a single room. This may express both the subordinate's wish for less supervision and his imagining of his future position as a boss in a privileged single room.

Q29 The majority of open-plan office users do not wish to have flowers, pictures and other decorations in their own workplace (five firms with 60 to 83 per cent). This shows the psychological tendency towards the rationalization of the working atmosphere in firms and is doubtless in accordance with the wishes of office layout specialists. However, this fact does not exclude the recognition of plant arrangements as a pleasant, less subjective way of enriching the aesthetic side of an office (Q26).

5.3 Output

Q30 The majority of open-plan office users find neither more nor less keenness for their work in the open-plan office, i.e. their personal attitude to work is unchanged; 77 per cent of the negative verdict open-plan office users in VIIa are less keen, and 52 per cent in VIIb.

Q31 Between 3 and 29 per cent of those questioned think that their calculable output in the open plan office has increased. However, not one of the 1,220 persons completing the questionnaires gave a figure for this increase. One cannot derive a value for increase in output from the proportion of workers stating an increase. It may be 5, 10, 20 or 30 per cent, but it will not be more than 50 per cent, because otherwise those questioned would have found it so considerable that they would surely have given some indication of amount. Similarly it will not be less than 5 per cent, because in that case it would have been too insignificant to be noticed at all. One may therefore put the value of the output increase —in so far as one wishes to attach any significance to employees' own remarks on increased output—at between 5 and 30 per cent. In any case the vast majority of those questioned in the majority of firms taking part are of the opinion that their calculable output has not increased:

55–90 per cent in firms II–VII. Even if—assuming one accepts these figures—15 per cent of those questioned have shown an output increase in the open-plan office of $\frac{1}{2}(5+30)=17 \cdot 5$ per cent; this only gives an average output increase over all the office workers in the open-plan offices of $2 \cdot 5$ per cent. This value must be considered totally hypothetical, however, because in the first place the above statements are not proof of an effective increase in output, and secondly such a survey is not equipped to ascertain output increases. One can only conclude from the answers a certain probability of a small rise in output in the open-plan office.

Q32 Only in the negative verdict firms do a significant proportion of open-plan office users think that they make more mistakes in their work. The majority of between 56 and 86 per cent of those questioned have found no increase in errors.

Q33 Between 29 and 73 per cent, on average about 50 per cent, of those questioned consider themselves more tired and irritable in the open-plan office—in the negative verdict firms the percentage is above the average. This is a remarkable and probably correct finding. Even in the positive verdict firms, which are apparently provided with good or adequate sound-absorbing devices and screens, a proportion of 29–43 per cent of tired and irritable employees must be considered disturbing and undoubtedly detrimental to general output. The accuracy of these subjective feelings can scarcely be doubted, even when applying extreme caution to statements of opinion of open-plan office users.

Q34 The number of workplaces that can be overlooked was given only by firm VII. It is clear that over-all visibility of the room is not considered desirable by office employees: the higher the number of workplaces overlooked, the less workplaces employees wish to see. The majority wish, common to all firms, to overlook fewer workplaces corresponds logically to statements that there are too few screens (cf. Q22).

In three positive verdict firms (I, II, IV) understanding for other departments has been increased by the open-plan office. There is no pronounced lack of interest in such understanding. The degree of interest ranges from the definite 'yes' of a majority of up to 86 per cent, through the 'indifferents' to a minority of uninterested.

Q36 Only in two concerns (I and II) do the majority of open-plan office users record a saving in journeys through the building. In concern VII, 31 to 62 per cent of open-plan office users state between 10 and 30 per cent saving in journey times. But a majority of open-plan office users in five concerns (III, IV, V, VII) deny any saving in journeys. If this is objectively true, then it may be attributed to inter-departmental relations, to the specific position of the department relative to the technical core, or to possible deterioration in communications, i.e. faulty organizational planning and space allocation. Just as probable, however, is the common subjective error that in a large open-plan office distances seem longer than in a large closed-plan office less of which is visible because of the walls.

Q37 In all the firms the majority of those questioned consider contact with workers in the open-plan office unchanged. This finding must be considered prejudicial to the hitherto contrary opinion of sociologists, psychologists and space planners; their only hope rests with the between 3 and 44 per cent—in one exceptional case, firm VII, technicians, 60 per cent—of open-plan office users who have noticed better contact with workers in the open-plan office. Contact with bosses has also not changed in the opinion of the majority of the office users.

Q39 Time-keeping of workers at the beginning and end of work has remained unchanged in the majority opinion.

5.4 Psychological effects

This part of the questionnaire only asks for subjective feelings. In order not to allow the answers to take the form of endless emotional outpourings, possible psychological effects had to be summarized and accordingly expressed as simplified formulae. No wording was used which would not be familiar to present-day employees. As at least 1–2 positive or neutral replies were provided for each question next to a maximum of 1–2 negative expressions, there should be no grounds for the objection that the person questioned might be influenced by the questionnaire.

Q40 The majority of the open-plan office users giving a positive verdict find it 'pleasant to live in'. This expression is selected by 61, 71, 78 and

80 per cent. Conversely the workers having a negative attitude find their firm's open-plan offices too bare (firms VI and VIIa). Firm VII is interesting: although all three open-plan offices are fitted out almost identically (and only VIIa and VIIc complain of too few screens), VIIa finds the room too bare, VIIb and VIIc pleasant. Doubtless it is not only screens and draughts from the air-conditioning plant which come into play, but also a different psychological climate within the same undertaking.

Q41 Those questioned feel largely unobserved by colleagues, at least the majority do not feel observed.

Q42 Nor do the majority feel disagreeably observed by superiors and subordinates. This refutes an important objection that comes up in every discussion prior to acquisition of an open-plan office that one is 'on display and continually watched by all workers'.

Q43 A small minority of those questioned feel lonely in the open-plan office. Neither mental security nor insecurity determine the open-plan office users' feelings: the vast majority of those questioned attribute scarcely any importance to this point. It therefore becomes unnecessary in similar investigations to place the greatest emphasis on psychological effects.

Q44 Only in three concerns (IV, V, VI) do a majority of slightly more than half feel 'one of a mass'. The majority of replies state 'member of a group', an effect which must be considered positive and intentional (a majority in three firms I, III and VII of 63, 55 and 69 per cent).

5.5 General verdict

The questionnaire asked for a general opinion from those questioned, all positive and negative impressions being weighed up to give a final verdict.

The following proportion of persons in the following firms considered the open-plan office better on the whole:

I	74 per cent
II	65 per cent
III	61 per cent
IV	60 per cent

VIIb   59 per cent

VIIc   64 per cent

The following workers in the following firms considered it worse on the whole:

V   66 per cent

VI   93 per cent

VIIa   71 per cent

It may be of interest to classify the positive and negative open-plan office users according to age, position and the types of office from which they originated: the results are shown in Table 5.1.

Table 5.1 General verdict on open-plan office according to age, position and office origin

Data	I	II	III	IV	V	VI	VII		
							a	b	c
50 Open-plan solution									
Better	74	65	61	60	15	7	28	59	64
Age:									
under 30	67	66	60	50	28	100	43	42	32
30–50	27	25	35	33	36	—	47	44	63
over 50	6	9	5	17	36	—	10	14	5
	100	100	100	100	100	100	100	100	100
Executives	23	15	15	22	5	—	21	23	17
Non-executives	77	85	85	78	95	100	79	77	83
	100	100	100	100	100	100	100	100	100
Formerly in:									
open-plan office	12	16	—	39	51	5	—	—	—
in 2–4 person room	33	23	45	14	15	50	32	31	21
in 4–10 person room	23	32	20	23	15	40	29	23	45
in single room	19	11	15	6	8	5	11	17	9
	87	82	80	82	89	100	72	71	75
Worse	14	17	15	27	66	93	72	37	36
Age:									
under 30	74	55	60	67	23	82	47	47	33
20–50	21	37	40	25	48	18	45	53	48
over 50	5	8	—	8	29	—	8	—	19
	100	100	100	100	100	100	100	100	100
Executives	—	18	20	25	12	7	23	3	16
Non-executives	100	82	80	75	88	93	77	97	84
	100	100	100	100	100	100	100	100	100
Formerly in:									
open-plan office	5	12	—	22	30	4	—	—	—
in 2–4 person room	37	43	60	11	25	11	51	33	21
in 4–10 person room	16	26	40	20	17	61	18	30	40
in single room	16	14	—	22	11	11	24	20	16
	74	95	100	75	83	87	93	83	77

171

The proportion of under 30's is greatest in the majority of the positive verdict firms. In two of three negative cases the proportion of over 30's and over 50's is more than double that of under 30's. Although this age composition expresses not only the degree of approval but also the general age composition of the firms and the open-plan office users, it is at least correct to say that in the majority of cases the majority of the younger staff—of up to 30—give a positive verdict on the open-plan office.

At the same time a large percentage of executive employees judge the open-plan office positively.

Office origin is divided almost equally between the positive and negative open-plan office users. One can conclude from this that in the long run office origin does not play any particular part in the verdict. Only in the initial period of use of the open plan will workers with open-plan experience have less difficulties than those coming from conventional offices. This difference is completely eliminated after a sufficient acclimatization period.

If one collates only the most important determining factors and only the decisive majorities for the general verdicts on the open-plan office, the picture indicated in Table 5.2 is obtained.

The reasons given in the questionnaires for positive or negative general verdicts on the open-plan office are predominantly related to questions of spatial design. On the positive side the modern and generous design and fitting out are particularly frequently mentioned. But even contact with workers and superiors, which is quantified in the questionnaires but does not rank either high or low ($Q37$ and $Q38$), appears (under $Q50$ and $Q51$) as a frequently mentioned positive reason. In the negative arguments distraction and disturbance are mentioned particularly frequently, which agrees with the quantification in the questionnaires (cf. $Q16$, $Q22$ and $Q24$). The frequent repetition of the resultant distraction and lack of concentration gives the impression of a serious argument, which shows up less in the quantified questionnaire replies ($Q24$) than when emphasized verbally.

$Q51$ The verdict on the employee's own workplace in the open-plan office is less strongly positive in the positive verdict firms and less strongly negative in the negative firms than the general verdict on the open-plan office. Nevertheless, the emphasis is clearly sufficient to show a definite order of positive or negative verdicts. Differentiating the verdict on own workplace according to age, position and office origin (see Table 5.3) gives a similar picture to that of the general verdict.

Table 5.2 Decisive (over 50 per cent) reasons for the general verdict on the open-plan office

Important data of the majority	I	II	III	IV	V	VI	VII		
							a	b	c
Positive	74	65	61	60				59	64
20 Sound absorption adequate	72	64		57					
21 Carpeted floor	96	79	89	99				100	100
24 Noise unnoticeable	75	54		59					
27 Free workplace arrangement	71	52	89	57				100	100
36 Saving in journey time	75	75							62
40 Pleasant atmosphere to be in	78	57	80	61				78	71
42 Freedom to move about	70	75	89	73				67	74
51 Own working place better	63	58	73					57	52
Negative					66	93	71		
20 Many office machines in the room					78	70	78		
21 Hard floor					78				
22 Too few screens						73	58		
23 Air-conditioning plant too warm						87			
24 Too loud:					55	73	60		
disturbance from passers by						84			
disturbance from conversation						73	75		
disturbances from office machines						80	80		
33 Exhaustion, irritability						73	69		
34 Too many workplaces in field of vision					54	90	73		
40 Atmosphere bare					73	70	50		
44 One of a mass					54	67	52		
51 Own workplace worse					66	83	59		

Table 5.3 General verdict on own workplace in open-plan office according to age, position and origin

Data	I	II	III	IV	V	VI	VII a	b	c
51 Own workplace									
Better	63	58	73	41	16	10	29	57	52
Age:									
under 30	65	67	46	50	26	100	52	41	37
30–50	28	24	33	29	36	—	38	51	58
over 50	7	9	21	21	38	—	10	8	5
	100	100	100	100	100	100	100	100	100
Executives	25	21	19	20	7	—	21	17	13
Non-executives	75	79	81	80	93	100	79	83	87
	100	100	100	100	100	100	100	100	100
Formerly in:									
open-plan office	14	17	—	41	50	4	—	—	—
2–4 person room	25	34	21	27	14	20	28	26	42
4–10 person room	33	24	42	16	14	66	35	32	23
single room	20	8	13	4	7	10	10	15	3
	92	83	76	88	85	100	73	73	68
Worse	23	19	12	50	66	83	59	23	31
Age:									
under 30	74	45	75	60	23	92	45	48	31
30–50	23	47	25	30	49	8	47	52	50
over 50	3	8	—	10	28	—	8	—	19
	100	100	100	100	100	100	100	100	100
Executive	6	18	—	26	11	8	23	16	22
Non-executive	94	82	100	74	89	92	77	84	78
	100	100	100	100	100	100	100	100	100
Formerly in:									
open-plan office	—	13	—	28	30	—	—	—	—
2–4 person room	39	37	75	12	25	12	45	16	17
4–10 person room	13	23	25	20	17	64	22	53	45
single room	16	18	—	18	11	12	27	26	22
	68	91	100	78	83	88	94	95	84

In the positive verdict firms the principal age group is under 30, in the negative verdict firms it is partly between 30 and 50. The proportion of executive employees is higher in the negative verdicts on own workplaces than in the positive. In those having a positive attitude to their own workplace the proportion of office workers with open-plan experience is greater than in those with a negative attitude.

Q52 The question on the management's reasons for choice of the open-plan office was intended to bring two facts to light:

1 How far are open-plan office users kept fully and accurately informed?
2 What subjective, fanciful ideas do open-plan office users have about management objectives, whether in spite of full information or because of incomplete information?

Evaluating the supposed reasons in decreasing order of importance

Table 5.4

Reasons for decision	Importance
Output improvement in work flow	10
Better supervision of workers	6
Flexibility of space distribution	5·9
Modernity	5·5
Saving in building costs	5
Publicity for the firm	4
Hobby of management	2
Other reasons	1

gives the order shown in Table 5.4. This imaginary order is certainly incorrect. For most firms the correct order would probably be:

Flexibility
Saving in building costs
Improvement in output
Modernity
Supervision
Publicity
Managers' hobby
Other

Improvement in output might well take first place, if there had hitherto been exact figures available for higher output in the open-plan office. Up to the publication of this work, however, it has never been exactly proved that output in the open-plan office is higher than in the closed-plan office. On the other hand the advantages of flexibility and saving in building costs are clearly recognizable and exactly determinable. Naturally it is not illogical to assume that the argument of increased output would have first place. However, the opinion in second place, that managements wish to control their workers' output more directly by means of the open-plan office, shows not only a misinterpretation of the situation, but also an atmosphere lacking in confidence in some firms (IV, V, VI). The misinterpretation of the priority of building costs is obviously based on insufficient informing of the staff (firms III, I, VIIb, IV). As it happens the saving in building costs in firms I and III was exceptionally great, and it is astounding that in spite of this failure to inform the staff, the open-plan office received such a relatively large vote (61 and 74 per cent) from the open-plan office users of these two concerns. Obviously the organizational advantages of the open-plan office in these two cases must be so considerable that they have compensated for the disadvantages of lack of information.

The majority of the positively orientated open-plan office users consider their management's presumed reasons valid. Two of the negative firms consider the presumed reasons (improvement in output and saving in building costs—firms VI and VIIa) invalid, which coincides with their own disbelief in the advantages of the open-plan office.

The positive open-plan office users express an interest in their firm, the open-plan office and their own workplace receiving a certain amount of publicity but the negative users do not.

5.6 Consequences

In not a single case have the positive open-plan office users remained with their firm because of the open-plan office, nor have the negative users remained in spite of the open-plan office; rather have both groups remained in their firms independently of their positive or negative attitude to the open-plan office. Even an open-plan office which in the employees' opinion is negatively designed or organized, cannot induce a notable number of workers to leave the firm. Even the influence of negative aspects of design in the open-plan office, which have been sufficiently discussed in detail in this book, is not sufficient to bring about such a serious consequence. This finding sets quite considerable limits on the importance of the main theme of this work.

Q61 Desired improvements are suggested by both positive and negative verdict open-plan office users. Better lighting is desired, particularly more daylight. Clear and unanimous is the desire for a more efficiently functioning air-conditioning plant. Additional sound-absorption is asked for repeatedly. Many want heavy smokers to be banished to a smokers' zone. Opening windows are requested, to let in fresh air (unfortunately this wish cannot be respected when there is an air-conditioning plant). Complaints are made about the electrostatic charge of synthetic fibre carpets. In some firms functional organizational planning is obviously lacking (VII). More generous space allocation and free workplace arrangement is wanted. Skeleton furniture is apparently not as popular as the manufacturers would like. Altogether the list of suggestions for improvement is instructive and worthy of attention.

A positive attitude of open-plan office users to the open-plan office is better than a negative attitude. Although it has not been proved that open-plan office users with a negative attitude give less output than those with a positive attitude, it does not seem improbable. The changing of attitudes from negative to positive can be achieved by technical and organizational measures and matters of staff policy.

An acceptance of existing office conditions must be considered as a positive sign. If office workers are satisfied with the present state, they will wish for a future state which is identical therewith (Q21 and Q25). This is not evidence of lack of a critical faculty. The same office workers demonstrate their critical faculty on other counts: they also wish for things that they have not got, e.g. a functioning air-conditioning plant (Q23) and more screens (Q22). Obviously the critical faculty is always present, but readiness to criticize varies. On important topics the workers are quick to exercise their critical faculty, e.g. air-conditioning plants, visual screening, screens, workplace arrangement, sound-proofing, disturbances, etc.; on less important subjects a certain poverty of criticism is evident; carpet colour, furniture material, plants, flowers and pictures, etc., apparently come into this category. This classification into important and unimportant issues is a subjective evaluation of open-plan office users. It is questionable whether office workers are in a position to appreciate the relative importance or unimportance of any one feature from an economic and organizational point of view.

The judgement of office employees must doubtless be rated more highly in the case of subjective findings, e.g. Q33—Feelings of tiredness and irritability, than in the case of objective factors, e.g. Q31—Calculable increase in output. Accordingly greater credibility, if not importance, should be attributed to all the statements on psychological effects than to the statements on output and fitting out.

Particularly useful and to be recommended is the attempt to replace subjective statements by simplified but methodical terms which can then be quantified. Double questions on the same subject confirm that one is justified in evaluating quantified statements more highly than verbalized expressions of opinion. For example, disturbances in the open-plan office are verbalized very strongly by all seven groups under Q50 and Q51, although according to Q24 only in two to four groups is there over 50 per cent objection to disturbance, resulting in a total negative verdict on the open-plan office in only three groups (V, VI, VIIa). In discussions and personal interviews, verbal statements often receive greater emphasis than is given to the judging of the same facts by the same persons.

Besides the numerous individual observations on technical and organizational details, there is one important fact to be learnt by managements about the open-plan office theme in particular and organizational innovations in general. Many workers think somewhat differently about what the management or organization and methods division considers decisively important when setting up an open-plan office: only in three concerns did the majority of workers name a correct, if not the clearest and most decisive, reason for making such a decision—improvement in output (I, II, VI). Not a single majority of open-plan office users recognized the main motives of managements and O & M departments for introducing open-plan offices—flexibility and saving in building costs. The workers' attitude to the firm is determined not by the effective objectives of the management or the stages of organization responsible for them, but by the subjective beliefs of the workers. These have to be influenced by moulding of opinion.

It is not enough to evolve objectives at the top. If the objectives are to concern every single person, they must continually be brought home to the workers by explanatory and propaganda measures within the firm until they penetrate the consciousness of all employees. It is not even necessary to impart the real objectives. People believe what they want to believe. Evaluation of the questionnaire shows (Q52) that the employees believe something which they have not been told and which does not correspond to the true facts. Well before the actual move into the open-plan office, the employees should be extensively and effectively informed about all the positive objectives intended to serve the interests of the firm and the persons working in it, until the majority of employees are convinced of the creative and productive basis of this new form of office organization.

If there is a generalized conclusion to be drawn from this survey, it is this: according to the majority of open-plan office users questioned in the majority of concerns tested, the open-plan office has proved itself. Is one justified in applying results from this minority of 7 firms to the majority of 40 concerns written to and about 1,200 not written to? Undoubtedly not. Although one cannot assume that the 33 other undertakings, judged by a wide consensus of expert opinion to have well-designed open-plan offices, refused to take part in the survey because their open-plan offices had been rejected or negatively evaluated by the majority of users—even if this possibility cannot be entirely ruled out—a vote by 7 undertakings can in no way be held to be representative for 33 other undertakings. Spatial organization, conditions within the firms and personal mentalities are much too variable. Seven or even forty undertakings are certainly not representative of 1,200 undertakings in matters of spatial organization. Other factors with a narrower range of effects, e.g. space requirements for records, use and profitability of office machines, type of work performed and forms usage, or the like—render it more possible to draw a parallel between a differentiated minority and the whole, than do complex problems, which moreover are just as much rooted in personal factors and environment as they are in rational considerations. The results of the present open-plan test cannot therefore lay claim to general validity for all existing open-plan offices.

Moreover, the test results do not constitute evidence of the general economic success of the open-plan office. The opinion of open-plan office users is neither the only nor the most telling criterion of open-plan office success. Up to the present only economic criteria—building costs, output and costs ratios, flexibility, etc.—can be considered as decisive yardsticks of the economic advantage of an open-plan office. In the normal case of an open-plan office with a uniform distribution of acceptance and rejection by the occupants, or even where there is a slight rejection majority (up to 66 per cent) which although not sufficiently developed to constitute a revolt is clearly perceptible, the profitability of the open-plan office can in the majority of cases—in the author's experience—be objectively and measurably demonstrated. These are lower building costs, rises in output, personnel advantages and other factors*. Negative opinions about the open-plan office are only relevant to the firm's economy if they decimate the productive capacity and efficiency of the staff beyond the average or result in mass resignation, sabotage or strike measures. Such a situation has not yet arisen and has not even been the reason for those isolated cases, in which the open-plan office has been reconverted into closed-plan offices at the insistence of the open-plan office users, or to be more accurate certain individuals in middle management. The objectively economic factors of the open-plan office should carry more weight than sociological measurements and statements of staff, the economic consequences of which are less clearly articulated and less easily measured. To this extent this survey is not the only or indeed the most significant contribution to the making of management decisions on this issue.

Nevertheless the test constitutes an important basis for discussion. It does away with misunderstandings, it supplies quantified numerical material on the sub-structure in seven concerns with 1,220 open-plan office occupants, and it demonstrates, in spite of its minority position, that with good design and organization open-plan offices can obtain the rational and emotional approval of their users and be recognized by them as a positive spatial solution. The minority scope of the survey does not detract from this result. Decisions should be made dependent not on the example of the majority, but solely on the rationality of the proposed solution. A single, logically postulated proof of success may be sufficient to justify following such an example.

* Cf. the author's remarks in Part A, Section 3.3.

BRITISH EXAMPLES OF OPEN-PLAN OFFICES

by B. H. Walley

Introduction

The use of landscaped open offices is gaining ground slowly in Britain and occurrences of the genre are still comparatively rare. It is perhaps curious that one of the examples which will be described has now the reputation of being a pioneer in the field, yet the final phase of the building conversion was occupied only in January 1968.

This example (the Building Design Partnership offices) is also significant because an already existing structure was converted to a landscaped open-plan office. The shell of the building, furthermore, might at first have seemed singularly unpromising as it was built in 1869 as part of a weaving shed.

The conversion has obviously been highly successful and despite some qualifications which will be discussed later, the outcome is a triumph for the skilled application of landscaped office principles.

Boots Pure Drug Company had a much larger problem on their hands, for they had to accommodate 1,200 office employees carrying out the complex headquarters operations of one of the country's largest manufacturing and retailing companies. In the context of an organization not noted for extreme radicalism (though it has some notable 'firsts') the design decision was highly adventurous. In five or ten years' time other major companies may have re-housed their office functions in more conceptually advanced buildings, but for the time being Boots is ahead of the field.

Building Design Partnership,
Vernon Street, Moor Lane, Preston, Lancashire

1.1 Introduction

Building Design Partnership in Preston has grown from a relatively small architectural office to a design unit employing approximately 190 people of various professions: architects, town planners, civil, mechanical and electrical engineers, quantity surveyors, graphic designers and so on. It also has a small accounts and administration section serving the whole firm, there being offices in London, Manchester, Belfast and other towns in Great Britain and in Johannesburg (RSA).

The offices previously occupied were above a series of shops in Preston. As more office space was required, extensions into adjacent property were carried out. Most offices had four to eight occupants; only two or three people had single offices. The premises had obvious defects, not least those which inhibited contact between the various professional groups.

It was decided that if significant advances in inter-disciplinary working were to be made, new office premises were desirable. However, there was a significant constraint in the limited budget which could be allocated for this purpose.

1.2 Concept

The principles of *Bürolandschaft* had been studied and it was considered that such an approach to office layout would have considerable benefits for the organization. A student was given a grant to go to Germany where he visited several companies and wrote a report in which he recommended the introduction of the landscaped-office principle in any new development which the company introduced. A house committee was formed to discuss the report and the partners eventually confirmed the committee's recommendation to go ahead with offices based on the *Bürolandschaft* idea utilizing an existing structure (after a further short visit to Germany). This structure had been at various times part of a weaving mill, a biscuit factory and a furniture warehouse and had a usable floor area of 23,000 ft².

For a design unit there were advantages in going ahead with this proposal. Conversion was obviously going to be much cheaper than building a brand-new office block. The purchase cost was £1.00 per square foot, conversion £2.00 per square foot and furnishing £1.75 per square foot. *Bürolandschaft* would cost less than converting such a building to a closed-plan structure. Not least there was the added attraction of utilizing their own office as a functioning example of everything that good modern office design should be. That this would help in establishing harmonious working relationships with clients requiring designs for contemporary office accommodation was not overlooked.

1.3 Over-all design

The shell of the building with supporting iron pillars, timber beams and large windows has been retained. The walls have been sandblasted to remove plaster and paint, leaving the brick exposed but suitably sealed. The main part of the building consists of two large rooms measuring 90 × 70 ft, one above the other and these have been designed as landscaped open offices (see Figs 7, 8 and 9). The lower of the two rooms has a ceiling height of 16 ft with a gallery housing an information and library section running down the middle lengthwise. The normal ceiling height of a landscaped office would be approximately 10 ft but this departure from design practice does not appear detrimental to the over-all appearance and function of the BDP building. The ceiling height of the first floor is close to the ideal 10 ft.

The ground and first-floor offices contain members of the various professional groups, while the administrative support groups which include secretaries with copy-typists are placed in the middle of each room to avoid reflection of typing noise from the walls. The initial layout for the ground floor and the first floor wing accompanies this chapter but following good landscaped office practice the layout has changed somewhat in accordance with current functional requirements, e.g. working groups associated with a major project have a team location. This obviously helps in the work of design. Both segregation and intermixing of professions take place depending on the current activities. Various segregated service areas comprising the central accounts department, photographic design and printing unit are located on

185

Main ground floor plan

Fig. 7

First floor plan

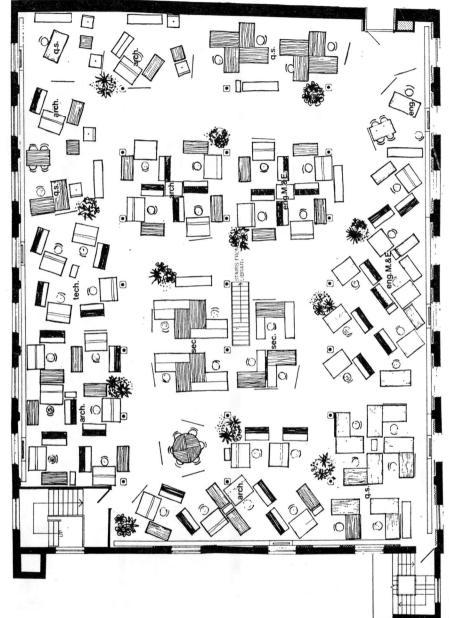

Fig. 8

First floor wing

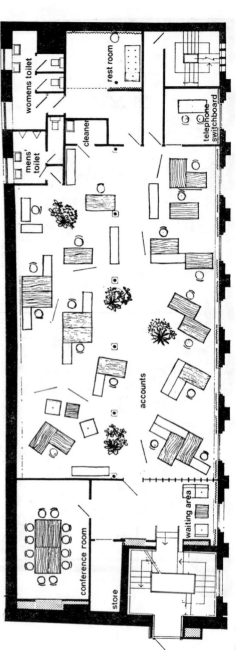

table

drawing
board

reference
unit

screen

additional storage
or filing unit

jacket holder

0   10   20   30 ft

womens toilet

rest room

mens'
toilet

cleaner

telephone
switchboard

accounts

conference room

store

waiting area

Fig. 9

three separate floors in an adjoining wing. Of these the central accounts department is also designed on a landscaped principle although it is only 50 × 35 ft.

The building does not lend itself to having a central service core and this may detract from its functional efficiency. The offices are smaller than those recommended by Axel Boje as being suitable for landscaping.

The general design of the offices was undertaken by Sidney H. Tasker, ARIBA, an architect partner in the firm, and other BDP specialists acted as quantity surveyors, structural engineers, etc. No outside consultants were used. This fact helped to ease the problem of communication of ideas and decision making and probably helped to reduce the over-all cost as well.

1.4 Design features

1.4.1 Air-conditioning

Air-conditioning, though considered essential by Axel Boje, has not yet been installed, mainly for financial reasons. Simple extract ventilation has been provided and fan convectors provide a variable amount of fresh air from inlets near the windows. Steps are being taken to improve the artificial ventilation as there have been problems on very hot days. Windows can be opened and staff take advantage of this facility.

1.4.2 Heating

Heating is by hot-water fan convectors and the air is ducted along the walls with exits by each window.

1.4.3 Lighting

An average of 60 lm/ft^2 is required from the permanent artificial lighting system. This is good, but by no means exceptional in modern drawing offices. It is increased by light from the windows which take up 40 per cent of the two long walls of the ground-floor office. Low winter sun penetrates 50 ft into this office and helps to give a bright, cheerful appearance. Nylon curtains can be pulled across the windows to exclude bright sunlight when necessary. The light fittings on the ground floor are recessed, 8 ft long, with Perspex diffusers.

At first-floor level the ceiling and lighting have been integrated in a coffered design so that the ceiling effectively becomes the light fitting,

189

throwing a diffused light from single fluorescent tubes down to the floor.

The coffered ceiling was more expensive than a normal, flat, acoustic ceiling but the cost was more than recompensed by the saving in light fittings, which in turn are more efficient because the need for diffusers has been eliminated.

Close attention was paid to the lighting of the central staircase although it is lit to less intensity than the office areas. All light sources are semi-indirect, utilizing existing recesses and other features in the walls. The stair tread is a light-coloured rubber and helps to avoid any noticeable decrease in light intensity when passing from office to staircase.

1.4.4 Acoustics

A noise level of between 40 and 50 dB was originally contemplated and this seems to have been achieved. Flat acoustic asbestos panels have been used on the ground floor and a coffered ceiling, described in section 1.4.3, was utilized on the first floor. The carpet must obviously play a large part in sound absorption. There is a scarcely audible hum from the ventilation equipment and this helps to avoid 'acoustical deadness'.

1.4.5 Furniture and fittings

Plants and screens are used to help to provide the appropriate landscape, but screens are rarely used to promote complete personal privacy.

The light-coloured birch plywood furniture was designed by Mr Tasker and is simple and inexpensive; it is a development of the BDP workplace which has evolved over 10 years. Only one of the partners has an off-standard desk. Generally there are no obvious status symbols which could immediately indicate the workplace of a partner or senior member of the organization (except additional space).

Groups comprising four architects and/or engineers form a convenient planning unit and furniture is placed accordingly. A member of the team has a desk, a storage unit and a drawing board plus the opportunity to utilize the reverse of a team colleague's drawing board, to form a four-sided workplace.

Quantity surveyors and secretarial staff have L-shaped desks incorporating storage units. Desks are designed to be assembled into groups.

BUILDING DESIGN PARTNERSHIP

The contract quality Wilton lime-green carpet is composed of 80 per cent wool, 20 per cent man-made fibre and is expected to last for seven years. It was the most expensive item in equipping the building. Lateral filing is in use throughout the building, in storage units which are either cupboards or files.

1.4.6 Conference room

There is a conference room available which would seat ten to twelve people round a table. This room has no window as yet, but following complaints about working in a windowless environment, one will be installed. Senior staff are emphatic that it is necessary to have windows in the building, to ensure visual contact with the outside world, if only to contemplate the weather. In some cases staff have turned their desks to face the windows.

1.5 Maintenance

Staff costs for maintenance and cleaning have been halved compared with those for the previous area of office accommodation which was less than a third in area. Simple dusting and vacuum cleaning are all that are required in the offices. There are hardly any painted surfaces.

1.6 Personnel attitudes

BDP is obviously one of those organizations where the difference in standards of accommodation before and after the occupation of the landscaped office has helped to gain acceptance of *Bürolandschaft* among the staff.

Turnover, usually an indication of high morale, is negligible—but it always has been in this firm.

The quantity surveyors seemed least happy with their new environment. The nature of their occupation dictates that they are often working against the clock to complete a project. Whether this job pressure, or the general environment, is at fault, is difficult to discern, but the outcome is a complaint that there are insufficient quiet rooms in the building which are free from distraction and where concentrated effort can be carried out.

Interviewing and conference areas are provided in the main layout.

191

These apparently caused some initial unease particularly when costs and job pricing were being discussed. There is apparently still reluctance among some employees to be completely frank in discussions in public. Other personnel take a contrary view and state that highly personal conversations are conducted without any inhibitions.

No psychological pressures or pre-conditioning of any kind were undertaken before the new offices were occupied. Factual discussions in which suggestions about the new office layout were called for, took place.

Slightly more stringent regulations concerning tea breaks have been brought in. At first personnel were allowed to visit a canteen in an adjoining building at any time between 10 and 11 am and 3 and 4 pm. Recently tea has been provided at work stations and now personnel carry on working, as they did in their previous office accommodation.

There is a very free and easy approach to personal touches at work stations—contrary to German practice. Pin-ups of various kinds are allowed. This does not seem to detract from the over-all attractiveness of the landscape.

Productivity is very difficult to assess in an architect's office and personnel are reluctant to claim that any improvement in output has been achieved, the most that is suggested is that productivity has been maintained.

1.7 Conclusion

Despite (and perhaps in some respects because of) differences from German practice, BDP has produced an exceedingly effective and pleasant version of *Bürolandschaft* on a slender budget. The wall texture is interesting; there is variety from room to room (differential ceiling heights, size of rooms and kinds of ceilings, for example) and there is an obviously less rigid attitude to staff than in many German examples.

BDP bears out the German evidence that office landscaping has definite cost and organizational advantages. Acceptance of the new office environment is very high. In many ways it could act as a prototype for larger organizations.

Boots Pure Drug Company, Thane Road, Nottingham

1.1 Introduction

By the early 1960s it had become evident that the labyrinth of offices in Station Street, Nottingham, was inadequate to function as the head-quarters of a large, efficient, manufacturing and retailing company. There were seven different buildings, one of which had once been used as a mill in the second half of the nineteenth century. They were too dispersed, too inflexible for organizational changes and obvious barriers to good inter-departmental communications and co-operation.

It was perhaps a surprise (not least to Boots employees) that the answer to the office accommodation took the shape it did.

1.2 Concept

When pressure of space and traffic problems began to force the consideration of new office accommodation, much thought was given to concept and design. One firm idea that emerged was that an office building could be both functional and beautiful at the same time.

An important element in the total concept was that the Lenton industrial estate is adjacent to the 300-acre complex of Boots factories and warehouses and the far-seeing founders of the company had bought land there which was still unoccupied. The site offered the best possible prospects for freedom of design, while on a more mundane level, car-parking facilities could be provided in quantity.

The extent of the chosen site provided enough space for a 'minimum height' building. Had a city-centre location been chosen, the obvious design would have been a high multi-storey block with space-consuming areas for lifts, stairs, service ducts, etc. It is claimed that usable floor space is approximately 80 per cent in the design chosen, while only 60 per cent of a multi-storey block could have been used for working purposes.

The site is seven minutes away from the centre of Nottingham by car and this factor possibly more than any design element initially provoked staff critics.

If 'the company a building keeps' is considered, then the general environment will never be comparable with Moorgate or the London city area generally, but it is still reasonably pleasant with a view towards the university and trees in the middle distance. The immediate site is obviously still new and once the trees and shrubs which surround the building increase in size, it will generate its own pleasant environment.

Four senior members of Boots visited the USA in 1964 to evaluate current office design. Many of the most satisfying yet functional structures seemed to have been designed by a firm of architects called Skidmore Owings and Merrill. A senior member of this company was asked to visit Nottingham to discuss the project and to see the site for the new offices. A London-based firm of architects, Yorke Rosenberg Mardall, worked in partnership with the American company and they designed the building jointly.

Boots provided the architects with full details of their requirements and how their organization worked. Visits were made to the original offices where inter-departmental communications, required storage space and office organization requirements were studied. Various possible solutions were suggested, the final choice being made by the Board in June 1965. Potential efficiency, flexibility, room for expansion and attractiveness were the main criteria. Boots personnel assisted in designing the office furniture, decor and general functional layout.

1.3 Over-all design

The building is set on a slight rise of landscaped grass, trees and shrubs. From a distance it appears to be a single-storey structure and it is not until the visitor enters the building that the ground storey is visible. This level has windows facing only on to a central, sunken quadrangle which is half an acre in extent, with grass, trees, a pool and three fountains.

The structure is supported by horizontal steel framing with floor to ceiling high windows on all except the outer walls of the lower floor. Altogether there is 214,000 ft² of floor area. A services core of toilets and cleaning closets, etc., is situated at each corner of the building on both floors.

Long office vistas have been broken up by the use of filing cabinets and numerous 'carrels'—flexible working units with wooden walls

5 ft 6 in high (the standard height for all the filing cabinets and carrels, etc.). The word 'carrel' is derived from a French word for a monk's retreat or a private room for study.

Surprisingly, perhaps, there are several private offices with smoked glass walls on the outer side of the ground floor. These do not provide complete privacy and some visual distraction must still penetrate to the occupier. The two computers have their own separate office, though programmers and systems analysts sit in the open office.

The use of *Bürolandschaft* has been eschewed for a rather disciplined layout of desks and office furniture. A less formal layout, it was felt, would be antipathetic to the full utilization of the space available and would make the provision of services—telephones and electric power— more difficult.

There are separate offices for the information section and library, the typing pool, the postal section, duplication services, the archives, etc.

There is a noticeable difference between the two floors. The ground floor has a 9 ft 6 in ceiling and has mushroom-headed columns 24 ft apart supporting the floor above. The first floor has no supporting columns and the ceiling is raised to 13 ft with windows on both sides and appeared to the writer to be a more attractive working area.

There is neutrality in the over-all colour scheme. The carpet is beige, the desks and movable walls of the carrels are natural brown oak veneer. A full-time gardener is kept busy looking after the welfare of the office plants which are provided as a colour contrast. It was anticipated that employees themselves would provide additional colour but this seems not to have worked out as well as it might.

Ceiling-high double doors cut off the directors' wing from the rest of the building. The directors' offices which lead off a corridor where their secretaries sit, are approximately 18 ft square. They face out over the car park, are comparatively modest (as befits any good company) and the difference in standards between them and the general offices is surprisingly small. (There is a general opinion that a levelling down of directors' and a vast upgrading of general office standards has taken place.) The psychological effect seems to be that directors are now much more approachable than they used to be.

Boots personnel are candid in saying that not everything has turned out successfully. The architects, for example, failed to realize that what they were designing was in effect a factory producing paper and provided inadequate access for paper and parcels, which has had to be provided subsequently.

There are seven 'coffee-shops'—areas in which tea, coffee or chocolate is allowed to be taken at any time from the vending machines provided. No chairs are supplied at the machines in the hope that refreshment breaks will be as short as possible.

1.4 Design features

1.4.1 Air-conditioning and heating

There are three air-conditioning and servicing plants on the ground floor supplying six changes per hour of filtered, washed and warmed or cooled air (20 ft^3/min per person). A thermostatic induction system beneath each window emits filtered air while stale air is taken away via extraction louvres which surround alternating light fittings starting 12 ft from the window, inwards.

The single, glazed windows can be covered by 250 electrically controlled blinds when necessary, so helping to eliminate outside light and temperature influences. The over-all control by temperature and humidity engineers has caused some concern. For example, the artists in the publicity department required less sunlight than those engaged on normal clerical duties and eventually the artists were given control over their own section of blinds.

Some complaints of excessive heat were heard in the summer of 1969, but once staff had walked to lunch in the temperature outside, complaints ceased.

A Honeywell control panel was installed to enable temperature and humidity readings at strategic positions to be taken at any time. Unfortunately, the sensors in some areas were found to give incorrect readings and now a normal wet and dry thermometer is used instead. There are local thermostats throughout the building which can be adjusted by engineers to give some local variation in temperature.

Steam for heating is obtained from Boots own nearby powerhouses.

1.4.2 Lighting

The lighting is designed to give an average of 60 lm/ft^2, similar to BDP. This, as previously stated, is not high by modern office standards.

The light fittings were specially designed and are spaced in rows 6 ft apart. Each unit holds one 5-ft, 65-W 'warm white' fluorescent tube. The reflector baffles are held in place magnetically and are easily detached.

The fittings are so arranged that at many angles it is impossible to see the light source, which aids the illusion of working in natural daylight.

Unlike a normal PSAL installation the lighting is operated by one switch per quadrant, i.e. a quarter of one floor, and it is not possible to switch sections on and off to compensate for the degree of natural light reaching into the interior of the office. The architects followed American practice derived from the idea that it is more economical to burn fluorescent tubes than to switch them off (and so shorten their life). So a quadrant's lighting has been left on for a single person working overtime, resulting in some high electricity bills.

The overhanging roof of the colonnaded terrace provides a shield against direct sunlight.

1.4.3 Acoustics

Noise levels appear to be less than 50 dB with punch card operators and typists in the office, largely due to the acoustic ceiling and the carpet.

The ceiling is made up of 5 × 2 ft acoustic panels, consisting of honeycombed glass fibre and asbestos.

1.4.4 Furniture and fittings

The architects moved against the current trend in furniture colour by advocating natural brown oak, strongly grained. All the furniture was built by Boots own workshops and the standard of design, flexibility and finish is extremely high. At first staff tended to scuff the finish on desk drawers but education and patience have now practically eliminated this problem, proof that staff will respect a good environment.

A variety of desks and filing arrangements have been made. In the carrels, for example, the 'desk' is actually a plain working surface which can be used as a conference table when necessary and all filing cupboards have been relegated to the sides of the carrel.

Filing cabinets in wood or black aluminium are fitted out according to need, but nothing stands higher than 5 ft 6 in.

Trailing cables have been avoided by having them embedded into the floor cavities and led up inside desks. These service points condition possible desk layouts.

The carpet is Brinton super-bell twist, 80 per cent wool and 20 per cent nylon, and is a tawny-beige. After two years' hard wear it has yet to have its first shampoo, yet is still remarkably clean. It is expected to last for ten to fifteen years, though some hard-worn sections may need to be replaced earlier.

1.4.5 Conference and training rooms and library information room

Training rooms have been designed and placed so that they have no windows or contact with the rest of the office. There are two training schools, one for wholesale staff and the other for the retail personnel, also a large conference room and adjoining display area or model shop. Experiments in display and shop layout can be undertaken in the model shop and the results are photographed and sent to branches, of which there are 1,700 in the UK.

Managers are encouraged to visit the information room which contains charts, diagrams and samples of new lines as well as press cuttings concerning the activities of the company and its competitors. The adjacent library section contains works of reference for all supervisory staff.

1.5 Cleaning

Cleaning costs are lower than in the old Station Street offices and cost approximately $17\frac{1}{2}$p/ft^2 per annum. The carpet is vacuum cleaned each evening. Anything that is spilt is dealt with immediately before it can become a stain. Fourteen men and ten to fifteen women are employed.

1.6 Personnel attitudes

Selling the idea of working in an open-plan office had to be intensive. 'Nobody wanted to move from the centre of Nottingham and nobody wanted to work in an open-plan office' sums up the situation. Yet the Station Street offices were poor from most points of view—desks, lighting, communications, etc.

Once the decision to move had been made and the design agreed, a model of a section of the proposed building, 48 ft long and 24 ft wide, was made. This was fitted out as a complete reproduction of the eventual working environment of the new office. This was then shown to the staff groups over a period of some months.

The model was supported by various artists' impressions of the new offices and these were posted in strategic places in the Station Street site. As the building began to take shape, busloads of the Station Street staff were taken out to see it.

All new staff are now given an illustrated brochure describing the offices in detail.

The move from the centre of Nottingham has caused concern, especially for staff who shopped during the lunch break for their families. This problem has been solved by providing a self-service shop on the site, where groceries and other foodstuffs can be bought. (The absence of 'cut-price offers' then became a bone of contention.) Shopping facilities have been extended on site by having a Boots shop where staff can buy at a discount. The lunch break has been reduced to 45 min allowing staff to leave at 4.45 pm.

Nottingham has a perennial shortage of female labour (Players, Raleigh, the lace industry—all extensive users) and Boots still has the same recruitment problem it had two or three years ago. It would be interesting to see, therefore, if the organized visits of local schools to the new office will help to close the recruitment gap by promoting it as an ideal place in which to work.

Productivity has not suffered from the move, but neither is a discernible rise apparent. The company is very largely tied to the local bus service and if buses are late then productivity suffers.

Absenteeism—the other criterion by which to judge morale—is also similar to that experienced when the company occupied the Station Street offices but there is a definite decrease in absences due to sickness.

Standards of dress and behaviour (always high) improved when the move was made and have been maintained.

The Office Council as the voice of 1,200 staff, has aired criticisms of the new building. These have tended to be minor and niggling—taps which refused to work and other small annoyances which might have been settled outside the joint consultation procedures. There have been complaints about the air-conditioning and the coolness of the offices generally so average temperatures have been raised from 68 to 71° F. (This bears out German experience.)

There is some discrimination between the different working areas. The ground floor with windows on one side was at first called 'the dungeon' and the directors' secretaries' corridor was called 'old maids row', by themselves, but there appears no malice in such terms. These probably are no more than early and temporary symptoms of staff adjusting to an environment which is not really under their control.

199

Over-all, staff have accepted the new office building. 'I wouldn't now change', and 'I like the spaciousness and feeling of luxury', and 'It's nice to think that this is one of the most modern office buildings in the country', are fairly common remarks. Deference in small degree to the closed-office idea has obviously helped this acceptance.

There seems to be a pride in the building which must eventually help to provide an environment for improved office efficiency.

1.7 Conclusion

Though radical, Boots offices are not completely revolutionary. It was perhaps psychologically impossible, perhaps functionally undesirable, for managers of all grades to sit and work in continual view of those they manage. The carrels and smoke-glazed offices provide a happy compromise.

Boots evinces a degree of discipline absent in the BDP concept and perhaps with such a high proportion of young female staff this is not surprising. The need for professional/technical groupings in BDP motivates a less disciplined form of control and layout. The difference in staff numbers is also crucial in this respect.

Is the building a success? By nearly every standard it is. It has proved its flexibility. Since opening early in 1968 till the end of 1969, 52 changes of layout have been made including the absorption of some Timothy White and Taylor staff following the merger, which had not been expected.

The atmosphere is relaxed. Office working conditions are superb. There is an air of quiet luxury about the building, the atmosphere of the lounge of a good hotel. Perhaps one could expect little less for the £2,000,000 which has been spent. It seems a good place to work in—an example to be followed.

References

1 SCHMALENBACH-GESELLSCHAFT, PETZOLD STUDY GROUP, 'Betriebwirtschaftliche Planungsgrundlagen (The Office—Management Planning principles)', *Das Büro*, V32 (1965).

2 SCHNELLE, E., *Bürobau planen* (Plans for office design), Hildesheim (1958).

3 ALSLEBEN, K., 'Die subjektiven Räume in einer Bürolandschaft (The subjective areas in a landscaped office)', *Bürotechnik und Organisation*, No. 6, p 513 (1964).

4 STIEGLER, G., 'Neues Grossraum-Verwaltunsgebäude in München (New open-plan administrative building in Munich)', *ibid.*, No. 5, p 435 (1966).

5 BAHRDT, H. P., *Industrie-Bürokratie* (Industry and bureaucracy), Stuttgart (1958).

6 SCHMIDT, –., *Bürotechnische Sammlung*, No. 89 (May 1962).

7 FUNKE, H., *Bürogebaude und Bürobetrieb* (Office buildings and office management), Hamburg (1965).

8 HERMKES, B., in LAPPAT, A., and GOTTSCHALK, O., *Organisatorische Bürohausplanung und Bauwettbewerg* (Organizational office block planning and building competition), Quickborn (1965).

9 MÜLLER-LUTZ, H. L., 'Die Kosten eines Arbeitsplatzes bei der Grossraumbauweise (The cost of a workplace in open-plan office construction)', *Das rationelle Büro*, No. 5, p 259 (1962).

10 HERTA MEYER-RIEKENBERG, 'Neun Forderungen der Gewerkschaft (Nine demands of the Union)', *Die Welt* (12 March 1966).

11 FISCHER, M., 'Von den Planungsgrundlagen bis zur Arbeitsplatzanordnung (from planning principles to arrangement of work positions)', *Das rationelle Büro*, No. 5, p 247 (1962).

12 SCHMALENBACH-GESELLSCHAFT, PETZOLD STUDY GROUP, *Kennzahlen neuzeitlicher Bürobauten betriebswirtschaftlich gesehen* (Data of recent office buildings from an economic standpoint), Duisberg (1960).

13 HANSMANN, W., *Kontor und Kaufmann in alter Zeit* (Counting house and merchant in olden times), Düsseldorf (1962).

14 HESS, C. W., *Bürobau mit Blick in die Zukunft* (Office building—a look into the future), Barmstedt (1961).

15 HENN, W., *Bauten der Industrie* (Buildings for industry), Part 1, Munich (1955).

16 PASSOW, C., *Lärm und Schall im Büro* (Noise and sound in the office), Barmstedt (1959).

17 KNIGGE, H.-J., 'Die menschliche Situation im Büro und die Arbeitsvoraussetzungen (The human situation in the office and working conditions)', *Bürobedarfs-Rundschau* (1961/62).

18 Noise Congress in Wiesbaden, *Welt am Sonntag* (22 November 1964).

19 GOTTSCHALK, O., *Flexible Verwaltungsbauten* (Flexible administration buildings), Quickborn (1963).

20 JOEDICKE, J., *Bürobauten* (Office buildings), Stuttgart (1959).

21 STUDIENGEMEINSCHAFT LICHT E.V. FUR FORTSCHRITTLICHE LICHTANWENDUNG (Research Group for Progressive Light Utilization), *Höhere Produktivität durch*

besseres Licht (Higher productivity through better lighting), Wiesbaden (1961).

22 BIELING, M., *Farbe im Betriebe* (Colour in work), Frankfurt am Main (1964).

23 RIMPL, H., *Verwaltungsbauten* (Administration buildings), Berlin (1959).

24 ANDREAS, D., 'Eine Untersuchung über Grossraumbüros (An investigation into open-plan offices)', *Deutsche Bauzeitung*, No. 6, p 469 (1967).

25 ZEH, J., 'Die Entwicklung des Bürohausbaues auch aus der Sicht der Baukosten (The development of office block building, including the building costs aspect)', *Voko-Kontakt*, No. 1, p 2 (1964).

26 LADNER, O., 'Ein Verwaltungshochhaus für die Zukunft gebaut (An administrative block built for the future)', *Das rationelle Büro*, No. 5, p 290 (1962).

27 SACK, M., 'Der Mensch ist eingeplant (Man is allocated)', *Die Zeit* (11 August 1962).

28 *Maschine und Manager*, No. 3, p 9 (1962).

29 LADNER, O., *Zweckmässige Arbeitsplätze im Büro* (Appropriate workplaces in the office), Stuttgart (1963).

30 RODIUS, H., 'Erfahrungen mit dem Büro-Grossraum der Firma Nino GmbH & Co., Nordhorn (Experiences with open-plan offices of Nino GmbH, Nordhorn)', *Das rationelle Büro* (28 March 1967).

31 HUMMER, H., 'Funktionsraumbüro—ein Fortschritt in der Büro-organisation (Functional area office—an advance in office organisation)', *Maschine und Manager*, No. 5, p 40 (1965).

32 SCHMIDT, H., *Bürotechnik und Organisation*, p 529 (July 1962).

33 ALSLEBEN, K., 'Beobachtungen in Grossraum (Open-plan observations)', *Das rationelle Büro*, No. 5, p 288 (1962).

34 FURRER, W., *Raum- und Bauakustik für Architekten* (Space and building acoustics for architects), Berlin (1949).

35 ROSNER, L., 'Das Grossraum-Büro (The open-plan office)', *Zeitschrift für Organisation*, No. 6, p 212 (1967).

36 DAG Paper, *Der Angestellte*, No. 1 (1966).

37 BELL, A., 'Was haben Angestellte gegen Grossraum-Büros (What employees have against open-plan offices)', *Die Welt*, No. 48, p 25 (26 February 1966).

38 CAMPHAUSEN, C. U., and PITSCH, I., 'Ein Platz für 100 Frauen (A place for 100 women)', *Bild am Sonntag*, p 36 (22 November 1966).

39 SOPP, H., 'Gedanken eines Psychologen zum Grossraum-Büro (Thoughts of a psychologist on the open-plan office)', *Bauen und Wohnen*, p 62 (February 1964).

40 SACK, M., 'Büro ohne Wande (Offices without walls)', *Die Zeit*, No. 9, p 8 (2 March 1962).

41 ROSNER, L., 'Der Büro-Grossraum hat seine zwei Seiten (There are two sides to the open plan office)', *Handelsblatt*, No. 220, p 11 (15 November 1961).

42 *Der Spiegel*, No. 39 (1965).

43 SCHNELLE, W., *Bürohaus als Grossraum* (The open-plan office building), Quickborn (1961).

44 ZELLER, –., 'Das Grossraumbüro als akustische Aufgabe (The open-plan office as an acoustic problem)', *Lärm-Bekämpfung*, V8, pp 113–19 (1964).

45 WELTZ, F., *Arbeit im Büro-Grossraum* (Work in the open-plan office), Frankfurt am Main (1966).

Bibliography

In addition to the books and articles mentioned in the References, the following books
and articles are also of interest.

ALSLEBEN, K., *Alle Umwelteinflüsse (Farbe) im Büroraum* (Environmental influences
(colour) in the office), Barmstedt (1959).

——, *Neue Technik der Mobiliar-Ordnung im Büroraum* (New techniques of furniture
arrangement in the office), Quickborn (1962).

——, 'Die Bürolandschaft (The office landscape)', *Das rationelle Büro*, No. 3, p 7
(1965).

——, 'Das Grossraumgebäude der Verwaltungs-Berufsgenossenschaft in der Ham-
burger City-Nord (The open-plan building of the Professional Association
administration in Hamburg City North)', *ibid.*, No. 3, p 24 (1967).

ALSLEBEN, K., et al., *Bürohaus als Grossraum* (The office block designed as open-plan),
Quickborn (1961).

BACH, F.-W., 'Der Raum—das wirkungsvollste Organisationsmittel der Büroarbeit
(The room—the most efficient means of organizing office work)', *Baumeister*, No. 7,
p 704 (1962).

BOJE, A., 'Wir stellen zu Aussprache: Grossraum oder Kleinraum im Büro (We throw
open to discussion: open plan or closed plan in the office)', *Maschine und Verkzeug*,
No. 2, pp 1498 and 1506 (1962).

——, 'Organisation und Komfort im Grossraumbüro (Organization and comfort in
the open-plan office)', *Das rationelle Büro*, No. 5, p 267 (1962).

——, *Moderne Arbeitsplätze im Büro* (Modern workplaces in the office), Düsseldorf
(1964).

——, 'Organisatorische Planung von Verwaltungsneubauten (Organizational
planning of new administrative buildings)', *Der Betrieb*, No. 16, p 1 (1964).

——, 'Der Verwaltungsbau des Centre d'Informations et d'Arts graphiques,
Lausanne (The administrative building of the Centre d'Informations et d'Arts
graphiques, Lausanne)', *Voko-Kontakt*, No. 1, p 1 (1966).

——, 'Der ideale Arbeitsplatz (The ideal workplace)', *ibid.*, No. 2, p 8 (1966).

BTS INTERVIEW, 'Der Mensch im Grossraumbüro (Man in the open-plan office)', Dr
Schmidt, Bertelsmann-Verlag, Gütersloh, *Bürotechnische Sammlung*, No. 5, p 1 (1962).

LE COURBUSIER, *Der Modulor* (The Modulor), Stuttgart (1953).

FÖRDERN UND HEBEN, 'Förderanlagen für Verwaltungen und Dienstleistungsbetriebe
(Conveyor installations for administrative and service departments)', *Technical
reports*, V12 (1967).

FORTUNE, E., 'Bürolärmbekämpfung durch Verwendung von Bodenbelägen (Combating office noise by the use of floor coverings)', *Das rationelle Büro*, No. 8, p 495
(1962).

FRANKENBERG, M., 'Die Neueinrichtungskosten eines Arbeitsplatzes (Re-equipping
costs of a workplace)', *ibid.*, No. 8, pp 471–472 (1962).

FRIELING, H., *Mensch + Farbe + Raum* (Man + colour + space), München (1954).

GOTZNER, K. D., 'Lärmbekämpfung im Büro (Combating noise in the office)', *Der Betrieb*, No. 16, p 34 (1964).

HEGE, W. H. J., 'Planung und Möblierung nach dem Prinzip der Wirtschaftlichkeit (Planning and furnishing on principles of economy)', *Bürotechnik + Organisation*, No. 5, p 388 (1967).

HENN, W., 'Die Aufgabe des planenden Architekten (The function of the planning architect)', *Das rationelle Büro*, No. 5, p 263 (1962).

——, 'Bürogrossraum und Architekt (Open-plan office and architect)', *Baumeister*, No. 7, p 655 (1962).

——, 'Hochhaus mit Bürogrossräumen in München (High building with open-plan offices in Munich)', *Bauen und Wohnen*, No. 2, p 63 (1964).

——, 'Bürogebäude in Rheda/Westfalen (Office building in Rheda/Westphalia)', *ibid.*, No. 2, p 69 (1964).

——, 'Verwaltungs- und Forschungszentrum der Osram-GmbH, München (Administration and research centre of Osram GmbH, Munich)', *ibid.*, No. 2, p 72 (1964).

HUNGENBERG, W., 'Die Kosten der Neumöblierung (The cost of refurnishing)', *Das rationelle Büro*, No. 8, p 457 (1962).

JACOBI, H.-P., 'Die Grundrisslogik eines Grossraumplanes (The ground-plan logic of an open-plan area)', *Bürotechnik + Organisation*, No. 10, p 834 (1966).

KLEIN, F., *Wie löst man Raumprobleme des Büros* (How to solve space problems in the office), Düsseldorf (1958).

——, 'Die Neueinrichtungskosten je Arbeitsplatz liegen zwischen DM 650 und DM 2,000 (Re-equipping costs per workplace are between DM 650 and DM 2,000)', *Das rationelle Büro*, No. 8, p 465 (1962).

KNIGGE, H.-J., 'Soziologische und pyschologische Probleme des Grossraumes (Sociological and pyschological problems of the open-plan office)', *Voko-Kontakt*, No. 1, p 8 (1967).

KNUT, F., 'Muss der Organisator in einem Einzelzimmer sitzen? (Must the executive sit in a single room?)', *Das rationelle Büro*, No. 5, p 298 (1962).

LADNER, O., 'Die Bedeutung des Lärmschutzes im Büro (The importance of sound-proofing in the office)', *ibid.*, No. 8, p 489 (1962).

LAMUNIERE, J.-M., 'Druck- und Verlagshaus Lausanne (The printing and publishing firm of Lausanne)', *Bauen und Wohnen*, No. 1, p 2 (1965).

LAUTER, C. G., 'Wo bleibt der Mensch? (Where does man stay?)', *Der Erfolg*, No. 11, p 537 (1966).

LÜSCHER, M., *Psychologie der Farben in Test-Verlag* (Psychology of colour in Test-Verlag), Basel (1949).

MANTHEY, M., 'Die Pyramidenbauer von Manhattan (The pyramid builders of Manhattan)', *Der Mittag* (23 and 24 August 1962).

MENGES, A., 'Zur Gestalt des Bürobaues (On office building design)', *Deutsche Bauzeitung*, No. 6, p 453 (1967).

MEYER-RIEKENBERG, H., 'Wirrwarr um das Grossraumbüro (Confusion about the open-plan office)', *Der Angestellte*, No. 1, p 2 (1966).

ORSOWA, W., *Der Betriebsleiter als Bauherr* (The business director as a builder), München (1966).

PALESKE, C. F. VON, 'Die Klimaanlage in einem Bürogrossraum (The air-conditioning plant in an open-plan office)', *Das rationelle Büro*, No. 8, p 485 (1962).

PRZEWOZNIK, P., 'Welche Fördermittel können in Verwaltunsbauten eingesetzt werden? (What means of convenience can be instituted in administrative buildings?)', *ibid.*, No. 8, p 507 (1962).

RENNER, P., *Ordnung und Harmonie der Farben* (Order and harmony in colours), O. Maier-Verlag, Ravensburg (1947).

REZNIK, H., 'Wie wir es gemacht haben (How we have done it)', *Das rationelle Büro*, No. 5, p 277 (1962).

——, 'Die Wechselbeziehungen zwischen Büroraum und Büroausstattung (The correlation between office premises and office fitting)', *ibid.*, No. 8, pp 446–56 (1962).

RHODE, H., 'Horten-Hauptverwaltung in Düsseldorf (Horten's main administration in Düsseldorf)', *Baumeister*, No. 7, p 675 (1962).

ROZENKRANZ, R., 'Muss ein Büroneubau wie ein Gefängnis aussehen? (Must a new office block look like a prison?)', *Das rationelle Büro*, No. 12, p 459 (1955).

——, 'Die Planung von Bürohausbauten durch den bürobetrieblechen Organisator (The planning of office blocks by the office organizer)', *ibid.*, No. 11, p 465 (1955) and No. 1, p 17 (1956).

——, 'Die Vorplanung von Verwaltungsgebäude-Neubauten durch den Organisator (The preliminary planning of new administrative buildings by the organizer)', *ibid.*, No. 5, p 231 (1962).

——, 'Zur Flächenermittlung bei Neubauten (On determining areas in new buildings)', *ibid.*, No. 2, p 37 (1966).

——, 'Rationelle Verwaltungsbauten (Rational administrative buildings)', *ibid.*, No. 3, p 7 (1967).

RUSS, A., 'Das Büro ins rechte Licht gesetzt (The office put in its right perspective)', *ibid.*, No. 8, p 499 (1962).

SIEGEL, C., 'Was kostet der Bau eines Bürogrossraumes? (What does an open-plan office cost to build?)', *Baumeister*, No. 7, p 667 (1962).

——, 'Gedanken über den Bürogrossraum im Hochhaus (Thoughts on the open-plan office in a high block)', *ibid.*, No. 7, p 672 (1962).

SCHARFENBERG, H., 'Grundsätze der Büroraumplanung (Principles of office planning)', *Bürotechnik + Organisation*, No. 1, p 7 (1963).

——, 'Durch sorgfältige Planung zu beispielhaftem Bürogebäude (By careful planning to the exemplary office building)', *ibid.*, No. 1, p 14 (1963).

——, 'Imposantes Hochhaus für 1000 Angestellte (Imposing high block for 1,000 employees)', *ibid.*, No. 7, p 608 (1966).

——, 'Barmenia baute beispielhaft (Barmenia buildings exemplary)', *Führungspraxis*, No. 8, p 26 (1966).

SCHEPP, L., 'Die zweckmässige Beleuchtung im modernen Grossraumbüro (Suitable lighting in the modern open-plan office)', *Der Erfolg*, No. 8, p 382 (1967).

SCHMITT, H., 'Einzelzimmer oder Grossräume? (Single-room or open-plan offices?)', *Bürotechnik + Organisation*, No. 7, p 529 (1962).

SCHNEIDER, X., 'Worauf es bei der Planung von Schriftgut-Forderbändern ankommt? (What is important when planning conveyor belts for paper?)', *Das rationelle Büro*, No. 8, p 512 (1962).

SCHNEIDER-ESLEBEN, P., 'Verwaltungsgebäude der Arag in Düsseldorf (Administrative building of Arag in Düsseldorf)', *Deutsche Bauzeitung*, No. 6, p 466 (1967).

SCHNELLE, W., 'Bürolandschaft—ein neuer Weg zu guten Büros (Office landscaping—a new way to good offices)', *Das rationelle Büro*, No. 5, p 255 (1962).

SCHRÖDER, K., 'Grossraum auch im Kleinbetrieb (Open plan even in small firms)', *ibid.*, No. 5, p 296 (1962).

SCHUSTER, K., 'Arbeitsplatzkosten im Bürogebäude (Workplace costs in office buildings)', *Bürotechnik + Organisation*, No. 5, p 398 (1967).

SCHWEINS, F., 'Grundsätze für Raumplanung, Raumgrösse und Raumbedarf (Principles for space planning, room size and space requirements)', *Das rationelle Büro*, No. 5, p 260 (1962).

SCHWEISHEIMER, W., 'Neugestaltung der amerikanischen Büros (Redesign of American offices)', *Maschine und Manager*, No. 4, p 28 (1961).

STEPKEN, L., 'Von innen nach aussen planen (Planning from inside to outside)', *Das rationelle Büro*, No. 5, p 256 (1962).

TIEDEMANN, R., 'Die Notwendigkeit der Teamarbeit zwischen Organisator, Architekten und Bauherren (The necessity for teamwork between organizer, architect and builder)', *ibid.*, No. 5, p 226 (1962).

——, 'Soll ein Neubau möbelmässig neu eingerichtet werden? (Should a new building be re-furnished?)', *ibid.*, No. 8, p 461 (1962).

TIEDEMANN, R., and MAYER, E. A., 'Möbelmässige Ausstattung von Spezial-Arbeitsplätzen (Furnishing of specialized workplaces)', *ibid.*, No. 2, p 16 (1966).

VIEREGG, J., 'Verwaltungbauplanung und rationelle Büro-Organisation (Administrative building planning and rational office organization)', *Voko-Kontakt*, No. 1, p 2 (1965).

ZOBEL, W., 'Verwaltungsgebäude der Nino GmbH in Nordhorn (Administrative buildings of Nino GmbH, Nordhorn)', *Baumeister*, No. 7, p 682 (1962).

Index